U0815174

全新数字经济

NEW DIGITAL ECONOMY

钱志新◎著

企业管理出版社
EMPH ENTERPRISE MANAGEMENT PUBLISHING HOUSE

图书在版编目（CIP）数据

全新数字经济 / 钱志新著 . --北京 : 企业管理出版社，2022.2

ISBN 978-7-5164-2277-9

Ⅰ . ①全… Ⅱ . ①钱… Ⅲ . ①信息经济- 研究 Ⅳ . ① F49

中国版本图书馆 CIP 数据核字（2022）第 015717 号

书　　名： 全新数字经济
书　　号： ISBN 978-7-5164-2277-9
作　　者： 钱志新
策　　划： 杨慧芳
责任编辑： 杨慧芳
出版发行： 企业管理出版社
经　　销： 新华书店
地　　址： 北京市海淀区紫竹院南路 17 号　**邮编：** 100048
网　　址： http://www.emph.cn　**电子信箱：** 314819720@qq.com
电　　话： 编辑部（010）68420309　发行部（010）68701816
印　　刷： 北京虎彩文化传播有限公司
版　　次： 2022 年 2 月第 1 版
印　　次： 2022 年 2 月第 1 次印刷
开　　本： 710mm × 1000mm　1/16
印　　张： 10.5 印张
字　　数： 172 千字
定　　价： 58.00 元

序 一

PREFACE

新的科技革命，其核心是数字革命，它已成为新世纪伟大的历史性变革。数字化正在重构人类的“三生”，即从数字化生活到数字化生产，再到数字化生命。数字经济是全新的经济，将为全球经济创造最先进的生产力，也是21世纪全球新的发展机遇。

一、中国改革开放以来，经济发展经历两大历史性变革，第一次是二十世纪八九十年代，从计划经济转向市场经济，社会生产力大解放，经济高速度增长，实现第一次历史性的大变革。第二次是从传统经济转向数字新经济，新经济推动社会生产力大跃升，经济高质量发展，中国将迈上经济强国的新台阶，实现第二次历史性的大变革。新的变革比前一次变革内容更宽广，成效更明显，意义更深刻。

二、人类正在进行两大迁徙：第一从互联网的线下向线上迁徙，扩展人类的发展空间。第二从物理世界向数字世界迁徙，拓展人类的发展维度。从物理世界到数字世界是向高纬度发展，因为数为高维代表事物的本质，数学原理为最根本的规律。任何领域一旦引入数学，就会实现认知的精细化，将从经验走向科学。

三、数字新经济的本质是经济的数字化，传统经济以实体为基础，新经济以数字为基础。数字新经济改变了经济的基础结构，基础逻辑的变化将改变一切，根本在于产业组织方式和企业生产方式的大变革。变革的核心是以数据驱动业务，实施“两个一切”，即一切业务数字化，一切数字业务化。所有实体经济都要建立新的基因，成为数字化实体经济。得数据者得天下，数据源为战略资源，中国有全球最大的数据源。

四、数字新技术为新经济的基石，通过数字新技术发展数字新经济。作为一个技术体系，数字新技术主要包括大数据、云计算、物联网、区块链、人工智能五大技术。根据数字经济的要求，大数据技术为数字资源，云计算技术为数字平台，物联网技术为数字传输工具，区块链技术为数字信任基石，人工智能技术为数字智能保障，五大数字技术是一个整体，相互融合呈指数级增长，推动数字新经济高速度、高质量发展。

五、数字化的最新发展是全面智能。人类社会从农业文明走向工业文明，现在正走向智能文明。工业革命是人类体力的大解放，智能革命将是人类脑力的大解放。全面智能的主体是发展智能经济，特别是发展人工智能，这是人类万年文明史以来最重大的进步。当今，正在加速走向智能新时代，麦肯锡研究院对智能时代与工业时代进行研究对比，呈现三大结论：从技术发展速度看，智能时代为工业时代的 10 倍；从经济规模看，智能时代为工业时代的 300 倍；从社会影响力看，智能时代为工业时代的3000倍。

六、智能经济主要实现“两化”，即智能产业化和产业智能化。当今最大的红利是智能红利，当智能化水平超过75%时，在不增加投入的基础上，GDP可达到现有水平的3.5倍，实现经济价值的最大化。对智能化的投入产出率高，1元投入，5元产出，越来越多的富裕人群来自智能新经济，足见智能红利的巨大威力。

七、新经济为新模式经济，新的模式不断涌现、层出不穷。主要的新模式有用户经济、平台经济、共享经济、服务经济和价值经济五大模式。这些新模式相互结合，产生众多新业态，创造大量新物种，充分体现新经济发展的多样化。最能代表新经济鲜明特征的是用户经济，新经济以用户为中心，因为数字能为用户画像，反映用户的本质需求，互联网在空间上零距离、时间上即时化，离用户最近。新经济模式属用户本位，一切围绕用户出发，强化用户体验，将用户需求放在首位。C2B是新经济最根本的定位，始终为用户创造价值，实现用户价值的最大化。新经济以“一体两翼”为最佳商业模式，在实体企业基础上增添数字技术和产业金融两翼，实现企业之腾飞。

八、新经济本质上是创新型经济。新经济以创新为纲，为创新劳动的代表，创新的意义超过以往任何历史时期。新经济以人才为本，将人才的创造力列在首位，个体的力量迅速崛起，强调人的自我驱动和自我发展。新经济呼唤新的领导力，领导力以价值观为根基，价值观的关键在于认知。领导者与领导者竞争力的差距最终表现为认知力的差距。认知力水平集中体现在两大方面：第一，对空间价值的认知，认知潜在的价值。正如冰山一角，在水上的小山，大家都认知，但仅为1/8，而水下的大山往往不为所知，却为7/8。第二，对时间价值的认知，认知未来的价值。现实的价值大家都认知，而未来的价值往往不为所知，其实未来的价值更远大。认知力是新的领导力。

九、数字化的根本不在于技术而在于新的思维，现在新思维与旧观念的矛盾已成为主要矛盾。当今新思维正在革旧观念的命，洗旧观念的牌，新思维变成新一轮财富之源，数字化将开辟全新财富时代。新思维的核心是创新价值观，重在彻底“换道”，不是在原来的道路上弯道超车，而是在新的道路上升维发展，走上数字经济的全新台阶。

十、数字革命是人类文明历史上最伟大的革命之一，数字革命使人类从低维走向高维，在高维层级上实现数字化生存和数字化发展。数字新技术的巨大作用是两大融合：第一，现实世界与虚拟世界的融合。现实世界为“阳”，虚拟世界为“阴”，成为双胞胎，两大世界的融合使世界变得更精彩。第二，碳基文明与硅基文明的融合。碳基文明为生物智能文明，硅基文明为机器智能文明，成为并列的双文明，两大文明的融合使世界变得更美好。数字革命起始于 20 世纪末，构建 21 世纪最大的新经济，到 21 世纪中叶将进入高级阶段，即全面智能的新时代。智能的大发展，加速社会的大进化，从更高维度开拓人类文明的全新境界。

我长期从事数字新经济的研究和实践，深感数字化为经济与社会带来无可估量的深远影响。20 多年来围绕数字新经济，我写过大量论文、微博、微信等，但大多是碎片化的知识，现在有必要进行系统化的集成。本著作旨在建立完整的知识体系，这对于数字新经济的研究和实践有现实的指导意义。

钱志新

序二

PREFACE

一、元宇宙溯源

元宇宙溯源需要研究原生宇宙。现实宇宙是由物质、能量和信息三部分组成的。人们一般认为先有信息，再有能量，然后才有物质。原生宇宙是一个超级的信息盘，且蕴含大量的信息。信息盘和能量盘结合产生宇宙大爆炸，产生能量并形成物质。众所周知，信息编码就是数据，所以原生宇宙充满了数据。数据是宇宙的一个本质，而“代码”是宇宙的“语言”。人类所有的开发，本质上都是在开发原生宇宙中的数据。这一逻辑是有根据的，一些科学家相信宇宙中有一种神秘的力量，而这种神秘的力量都是由数字和公式组成的，这种神秘的力量统治整个宇宙。这种认知说明确实存在着一个原生宇宙，就是一个以数字为中心的宇宙，人们通过开发原生宇宙，得到很多新的发现。元宇宙和现实宇宙是高维和低维的关系，现实宇宙是三维的，再加上时间就是四维的。而元宇宙是四维以上的，它超越了时空。元宇宙是高维主导低维的发展，主要是超级信息量的作用。因此，元宇宙为原生宇宙的超级信息盘发展而来的，元宇宙和现实宇宙相比是高维主导低维的关系。

二、元宇宙规则

元宇宙有自身的规则，这些规则超越现实宇宙的诸多限制。人们从四个维度来考查元宇宙的规则：第一，创造为本。元宇宙的主题是创造为本，创造驱动一切，不同于实体经济社会以生产为中心，元宇宙以创造为中心，这种创造力是由自由创造者通过计算来形成的。第二，虚拟社区。元宇宙的组织不同于传统经济组织形态，传统组织主要是公司，经济组织以公司为基本单元，但元宇宙的组织是一个虚拟社区，我们称之为 DAO。DAO 实际上是一个数字化的社群，它是去中心化的，在 DAO 里面实现自我管理。DAO 就是自由人的联合体，可以按照自己的需求、兴趣、行为和爱好组织起来。一个主体可以参加许多 DAO，DAO 就是一个自治的合作组织。第三，“四共”机制。(1)“共”是共创，就是大家共同创造，共创就是生产力；(2)“共”是共享，创造的价值都是共享的，共享就是生产关系；(3)“共”是共治，在 DAO 这个合作组织里面是主体自治的，共治就是新的上层建筑；(4)“共”是共荣，在 DAO 里面是大家共同享受这种荣光的，这是一种新的价值观。第四，无限发展。为什么会无限发展呢？因为它的边际成本为零。数据有两个特点：(1)数据是无限的，根据新的摩尔定律，也就是说数据每 18 个月翻一番，所以数据是无限的；(2)数据可以无限复制。由于这两个特点，所以元宇宙的发展是无限的。物质资源是有限的，数据资源是无限的。数据复制的边际成本为零，边际效应也是递增的，不是递减。这四个规则与现实社会不一样，但是这四个规则很重要，说明元宇宙里面的很多限制和界限都被打破了，所以发展更自由。

三、元宇宙要素

元宇宙由数字身份、数字产品、数字资产、数字市场和数字货币五大要素构成。第一个要素是数字身份。数字身份是进入元宇宙的前提条件，我们要进入元宇宙需要借助于数字化身，数字化身进入元宇宙后可以自我学习、自我成长、自我迭代、自我进化。第二个要素是数字产品。元宇宙中数字产品都是内容产品，也可以将实体产品转化为数字产品，还可以由人工智能创造数字产品。数字产品创造的渠道很多，一是数字化身创造了数字产品；二是把实物产品数字化；三是人工智能(AI)创造数字产品。第三个要素是数字资产，元宇宙的资产是数字资产。常见的数据、软件系统都是数字资产，同时实物资产也可以转化为数字资产。相信今后的数字资产大于实物资产，且数字资产不同于实物资产的一个重要特征是，实物资产会不断贬值，而数字资产不会贬值反而会增值。第四个要素是数字市场。在元宇宙中进行数字产品和数字资产交互的场所称之为 NFT。第五个要素是数字货币。人们通常把在元宇宙的数字货币叫作通证，可以分成两种：一是数字货币的通证；二是数字资产的通证。其中数字资产的通证是有内容的，所以现在数字资产 NFT 是允许和支持的，纯粹地搞比特币是不支持的，这里就有这样的一个区别。数字货币是客观存在的，现在人民币本身也开始数字化，在海南要建立一个数字人民币的市场。也就是说，数字货币是能够流通的。

四、元宇宙技术

元宇宙技术是数字技术的集大成，主要包括大数据技术、人工智能技术、区块链技术和虚拟现实技术。第一是大数据技术。元宇宙是由数据构成，大数据是元宇宙中最好的资产。它采用分布式存储，先将一个数据包打碎，用的时候再进行复原。所以元宇宙里数据是最安全的，分布式存储是元宇宙里面重要的技术措施。第二是人工智能技术。它是元宇宙里面的核心技术，真正的数字产品、数字资产就是通过人工智能产生的，没有人工智能就产生不了数字产品，产生不了数字资产。第三是区块链技术。区块链可以明确数据的产权，可以帮助实现数据流通、交换、交易和增值。区块链还具有两个重要机制：一是共识机制。共识机制就是在一个组织里面，各个主体形成的一个规则，来共同遵守。二是智能合约。通过智能合约实现价值智能分配。第四是虚拟现实技术。虚拟现实技术是进入元宇宙的工具，到元宇宙的入口有两种：第一是 VR、AR 和 MR，虚拟现实的设备，最近很流行，比如数字眼镜、数字头显等。第二路径是脑机接口，把大脑和电脑对接好，马斯克搞了脑机接口，脑机接口如果进了元宇宙，那就更加的无障碍了、更直接了，体验性就更好了。因此，大数据技术、人工智能技术、区块链技术和虚拟现实技术连贯起来构成一个完整的体系。大数据是元宇宙的资源；人工智能技术是元宇宙的生产力；区块链把内容变成价值；虚拟现实是进入元宇宙的工具。

五、元宇宙应用

元宇宙的应用非常重要，也非常广泛，这里主要举七个领域的案例来介绍元宇宙的应用，分别是：游戏、社交、艺术、教育、设计、营销和产业。第一个应用是游戏。因为游戏相对简单，而且容易打开市场，找到受众。最近旅游数字化也很火，杭州西湖十八景，每一个景点都搞成一个元宇宙的数字产品，比你身临其境体验性还要好，比你自己亲自去，更感到沉浸化。第二个应用就是社交。要发展数字化社交，不同实体的社交，数字人在元宇宙中进行社交，可以在元宇宙中交换元宇宙的产品，交换元宇宙的资产，使产品和资产增值。元宇宙的社交是超越了时空的。如果我们到元宇宙中召开视频会议，那就不同于现在的腾讯视频会议，可以把每个人的数字化身全部集中到一个空间，可以让参会人感觉和真实会议室的感觉一致。这种社交也是超越了时空的。第三个是艺术品。如何让更多的艺术爱好者欣赏或收藏到故宫里的艺术品。我们可以开发一个数字版的故宫艺术品，以满足更多人的需要。不光是艺术品，还有歌唱家，歌唱家也可以到元宇宙中去歌唱，比如说已经去世的一些歌唱家，根据他们原来的视频和音频，我们把它们复原以后，变成一个数字化的歌唱家，照样可以唱一系列现代歌曲。这样文化艺术也就走向了元宇宙。第四个应用是教育。元宇宙将使教育的体验性更强，开展沉浸式的教育。比如现在学校里做实验，如果搞数字化的实验，我们也可以带回家去做。给你一套数字化的产品，想做多少次都可以，这样你的兴趣就不一样了。再比如医学院的学生怎么样来临床实习，看真正的病人是成本很高的，现在搞一个数字化病人给你看，有患癌症的，患糖尿病的，你天天看就懂了。所以元宇宙在教育上应用是非常广泛有效的。第五个是设计。设计更加需要元宇宙，传统的设计往往是设计人在家里冥思苦想地设计，而现在可以先搞数字模型，再去搞实体的产品。比如北京大兴机场的修建，是通过先构建一个机场整体建设的数据模型，并征求三方面意见：一是征求领导的意见；二是征求专家的意见；三是征求客户的意见。三方面意见集中起来，反复改了多次，最后达成共识，形成最终的建设方案。这一过程大大降低了成本，减少了返工，缩短了工期。第六个是数字营销。现在做数字主播非常流行，数字主播具有很多优势，比如可以不知疲倦连续工作，可以在不同场合同步直播，覆盖面大，所以现在数字营销非常流行。还有就是数字产品和实体产品的互动，比如在元宇宙里数字产品卖得比较好，实体就赶快做起来。反过来，有一个实体产品卖得比较好，就带到数字空间去。两个互动以后，本来是一个市场，变两个市场了。这样就是虚拟和实体的营销互动，带动企业的营销。第七个是产业应用。所有的产业都可以搞元宇宙，搞数字孪生、数字双胞胎。比如把一个工厂里所有的场景，复制到元宇宙里搞个数字场景，之后这个数字双胞胎再用元宇宙里的数据进行优化，很多数据在元宇宙里面，实体是没有的，反而元宇宙里的数据大大超过我们实体里面的数据。所以数字双胞胎能吸收元宇宙里大量数据，吸收了这些数据以后不断地迭代优化，优化以后产生新的价值再回到实体场景中去，这样就实现了增值。所以，今后工厂都要元宇宙化的。元宇宙将会渗透到每一个产业、每一个企业中去，未来十年是元宇宙的黄金十年。

六、元宇宙财富

第一个是价值。认同决定价值，元宇宙里的价值确定不同于实体的价值确定方法。实体价值是通过市场来确定，或者是用户确定的，或者是企业确定的；而在元宇宙中则是由认同来决定价值。在元宇宙中，大家都认同这个东西值1000块钱，那它就值1000块钱。它不用到市场上去竞争，它的价值在这个数字社群会被大家认可并接受，而且这种定价机制可以通过智能合约来自动实现。第二个叫UGC，什么叫UGC呢？用户来创造内容，在元宇宙里，用户是三个概念，用户是内容创作者，也是消费者，又是交易者。三个是在一起的，是自由的。第三个是NFT。用于数字资产交易，通过区块链来储存、流通、交易、激励和增值。元宇宙里的财富和现实世界财富不是一个数量级的。凡是进入一个新的技术开拓的市场，大体上有三个阶段：第一阶段，有1%到37%的人先发效应，这个财富是很快能拿到的。第二阶段，37%到70%这一段就竞争激烈了，你这个财富效应就差了。第三阶段，70%以后基本没有财富效应了，所以现在这个投资界都要抢占元宇宙这个跑道，就是要抢在37%之前要进去，现在只有3%的渗透率，到37%还早，所以现在进入元宇宙正是好时机。

七、走向元宇宙

第一个观点是“大迁徙”。第一次迁徙是人类从非洲大陆迁徙到其余各个大陆去，到欧洲、亚洲和美洲。第二次迁徙是从大陆到海洋，到海洋去的都是大进化。第三次迁徙是从海洋到太空，现在马斯克将要到太空去。第四次迁徙就是从物理世界走向数字世界，这一次大迁徙是人类历史上最大的一次迁徙，也是最大的一次进化，它将开拓人类发展的新的维度，它是从更高的维度来发展。第二个观点是人类是不断迁徙的，每一次迁徙都是大的发展。从物理系统到数字系统，这两个系统是走向一体化的，不是割裂的。元宇宙不是虚拟世界，也不是实体世界，它是虚拟和实体融合的全新世界。所以，大家不要认为元宇宙很空，看不见摸不到，它既不是虚拟世界，也不是实体世界，它是虚拟和实体一体化融合起来的世界，虚实共融，以虚驭实，数字起到主导作用，通过数字世界为物理世界升维，使物理世界指数级地增长财富。我们一定要理解元宇宙的思维和元宇宙的机制，而不是简单地搞元宇宙的技术。有人认为元宇宙已经有泡沫了，新事物成长过程中，泡沫是进步的代价，没有泡沫就不能进步。泡沫结束以后，新的、优秀的企业就留下来了，就走向了一个新的发展阶段。互联网也是这样，在 20 世纪 90 年代末的时候，互联网很兴旺，但是到 2000 年的时候，它出现了泡沫。泡沫过去后，现在还是很兴旺。所以元宇宙有泡沫，但不能因为它出现了泡沫就不发展了。优胜劣汰法则可以让优秀的企业和实体生存下来。第三个观点，我们认为元宇宙是新的文明，元宇宙是数字化发展的必由之路。元宇宙是数字技术的大集成，数字技术都会在元宇宙体现。元宇宙是数字经济的高形态，数字经济的最高形态就是元宇宙。元宇宙是数字社会的新空间，数字社会是无限发展的新空间。这三个观点标志着我们人类走向数字发展的新文明。

钱志新

目录

CONTENTS

第一部分　数字之魂

Part One　The Soul of Digital

第二部分　数字经济

Part Two　Digital Economy

数为本之源，数化万物；

智为数值流，智融天下。

Digit as the source of essence composes everything;

Intelligence representing the numerical flow integrates the world.

数字新经济的内涵有两大部分：第一以数字技术为核心的数字经济；第二以数字为基础的新经济模式。两者融合构建数字新经济。当今，数字技术加速发展，呈现指数级增长，推动数字新经济成为最强大的社会生产力。

The connotation of the digital new economy has two major parts: the first is the digital economy centering on the digital technology; the second is the new economic mode with digital economy as the leading factor. The two integrate with each other in order to build a digital new economy. Nowadays, the development of digital technology is accelerating and showing exponential growth, promoting digital new economy to be the most powerful social productive forces.

第一部分　数字之魂
Part One　The Soul of Digital

人类已进入数字大时代，从生产力角度来考察，工业革命以来经历了四次大变革：第一次是 18 世纪以蒸汽机为代表的机械化；第二次是 19 世纪以电力为代表的电气化；第三次是 20 世纪以计算机为代表的信息化；第四次是 21 世纪以人工智能为代表的数字化。数字时代是与农业时代、工业时代并列的三个大时代，人类将从无限劳动力走向无限计算力，由无限计算力迸发无限创造力。

At present, mankind has been in the digital era undoubtedly, which has undergone four major changes form the perspective of productivity since the industrial revolution. Firstly, mechanization represented by the steam engine in the 18th century; Then, electrification represented by electricity in the 19th century, followed by information with computers in the 20th century; Lastly, the digitization represented by artificial intelligence in the 21st century. The digital age is one of the three major times, along with the agricultural age and the industrial age. Mankind will move from infinite labor to computing power, which will unleash infinite creativity.

一、数字之源

The Source of Digital

宇宙的本源为数，全息理论认为宇宙大爆炸以前是全部信息盘，即超级数据库。宇宙中充满着数，数是宇宙间的通用语言，成为宇宙中的灵魂。

The origin of the universe is digital. Holographic theory holds that the universe was all information disk before the Big Bang, namely super database. Generally speaking, the universe is full of digital and most common language is digital.

1. 万物皆数

古代哲人毕达哥拉斯认为“万物皆数”。量子世界中“弦”为最小单位，其振动频率为数；生物基因中“ACGT”四个密码都是数；中国周易也认为“易经之源为数”。世界上许多数字是永恒的，如圆周率为“π”(3.1415…)，黄金分割率 0.618 为宇宙之钥匙。总体来说，万物表示存在方式，数字代表根本属性，数字与万物是一体两面、不可分割的，数为本源。

1. All is Number

The ancient philosopher Pythagoras believed that all is number. In the quantum world, the string is the smallest unit with a number of vibration frequencies and the four codes of "ACGT" in biological genes are all numbers. Meanwhile, The Book of Changes also considered that the l Ching is based on numbers. Actually, there are many eternal numbers in the world such as π(3.1415…) and the golden ratio is 0.618, which is the key to the universe. Generally, all things represent the way of existence, while numbers the fundamental attributes. Numbers and all things on earth are two sides inseparably. Totally we can say that number is the source and the soul.

2. 万物关系为数字关系

万物之间的关系都是数字关系，数学原理为最根本的原理。万物相互关系最简单的表达方式是数学公式，它揭示了宇宙发展的科学规律。对伟大科学家终生成就最好的表达就是数学公式，如牛顿的 $F=ma$，爱因斯坦的 $E=mc^2$。数学公式是算法之本质。

2. The Relation of All is a Number Relationship

The relationship between all things is a number relationship so that the principle of mathematics is the most fundamental. Among them, the mathematical formula is the simplest expression of the relationship, which reveals the scientific law of the development of the universe. The best expression of great scientists' lifetime achievement is the mathematical formula such as $F=ma$ of Newton and $E=mc^2$ of Einstein, which is the essence of algorithms.

3. 数字世界与物理世界

人类是不断迁徙的,并正从物理世界向数字世界迁徙,以拓展人类的发展维度。从原子世界走向比特世界,核心数字是 0 与 1,大量比特数字的集合构建数字世界的一切。数字世界是一个全新世界,数为高维度,引领低维度发展,将从根本上改变物理世界的观念和规则,开拓前所未有的认知世界。物理世界是分布式的,数字世界是集合型的,数字的集成整合产生全新的价值,化不确定性为确定性,实现指数级发展。数字世界与物理世界是融为一体的,数字孪生是两个世界的双生子,数学模型在先,指导物理实体。

3. The Digital and Physical Worlds

It is well known to us all that human beings are migrating constantly. They are from the physical world to the digital world now, for example, to expand the dimensions of human development. From the atomic world to the world of bit, where the core numbers are zeros and ones, the vast collection of bits that contribute everything in the digital world. It is a brand new world that number is a high — dimensional guide to low one and a higher dimensional development belongs to its essence, which will fundamentally change the concept and rules of the physical world and race an unprecedented cognitive world. The physical world is distributed, while the digital one is collective. The new value comes from the integration of numbers, which turns uncertainty into certainty and achieves exponential development. However, the two worlds are integrated because of the digital twins of them, in which the mathematical model comes first, guiding the development of the physical entity.

二、数字之道

The Way of Digital

万物皆数，数重构万物的基础结构，此即数字之道，根本上是改变世界的发展方式，一切将重新定义。

All is digital, and it reconstructs the infrastructure of all things inversely. It means that the way of digital will transform the world development mode radically, redefining everything.

1. 数字化本质

数字化本质是变革基础结构，从物质为基础转变为以数字为基础，数字成为底层逻辑。数字化的首要问题是业务与数字的关系，所有业务都是表象，其本质都是数字，要从数字这个根基上解决复杂的业务问题。数字化的机制是数据驱动业务，首先将业务转化为数据，不同的业务变成同质的数据，通过各种数据的聚集、整合和建模，产生新的价值，然后返回到业务中去，最后使业务增值。概括其过程为“两个一切”，即一切业务数据化，一切数据业务化，形成闭环增值。数据从业务中来，回到业务中去，数据业务化实现更大价值。

1. The Essence of Digitization

The essence of digitization is the infrastructure that changes the world, from material－based to digital－based with it as the underlying logic. The reason why the primary problem of digitization is the relationship between service and digital is that all services are on the surface. It is undeniable that its essence is all digital, so it is necessary to solve complex business problems from the root of digital. Data － driven business is a digital mechanism that transforms business into data firstly and different services become the same data to generate new value through the aggregation, integration and modeling of various data. Finally, it will return to the services and appreciate in value. In a nutshell, the process contains the digitization of service and the data operationalization, which is called two everything, to realize closed－loop value－added. Therefore, the data comes from the service and back to it ultimately for the better value of data operationalization.

2. 数字化与“三化”

数字化与信息化、网络化、智能化的关系，从总体上都属于数字化。数字化是信息化的升级，信息化以业务为主导，数据为辅助；数字化以数据为主导，业务为载体，主导面发生了根本性改变。数字化覆盖网络化，网络化仅为数据的连接、传输和协同。数字化的高级阶段为智能化，数字为智能之源。所谓智能，其本质是对变化的适应性，通过大量数据的洞察和处理产生智能，适应和预判现实世界的不断变化。麦肯锡研究院对智能化与工业化作比较研究，认为智能化的科技发展速度是工业化的数十倍，智能化的经济规模是工业化的300倍，智能化的社会影响力是工业化的3000倍。这就是智能化的巨大威力。

2. Digitization and Informatization, Networking, Intelligence

Digitization, informatization, networking, and intelligence are all digital. Digitization is the upgrading of informatization, which is dominated by service and assisted by data. At the same time, digitization takes data as the leading factor and regards the service as the carrier, that is to say, the dominant aspect has undergone fundamental changes. Digitization covers networking, which is only the connection, transmission and collaboration of data. The advanced stage of digitization is intelligence and the digital of the source of intelligence. The essence of intelligence is the ability to anticipate and adapt to all changes through the insight and processing of large amounts of data. The McKinsey Research Institute conducted a comparative study of intelligence and industrialization deeming that the speed of intellectualized science and technology development is dozens of times that of industrialization, while the intelligent economy is 300 times that of industrialization, and influence of society has reached 3000 times of industrialization, which is the huge power of intellectualization comparative study of intelligence and industrialization.

3.数字思维

数字化的核心是数字思维,数字思维集中起来主要有五大思维:第一,数据思维,应充分相信数据的力量,数据大于逻辑,得数据者得天下,关键要确立数据价值观。第二,客户思维,数字化以客户为中心,客户社区是最大的资产,经营客户是经营之根本,客户就是价值网,要不断与客户互动,为客户服务是无止境的。第三,链接思维,数字化全在于链接,链接大于本体,链接越多,资源越多,机会也越多。通过链接将业务上网、上云、上链,实现线上与线下一体化。第四,平台思维,数字化为平台模式,构建“平台+个体(小团组)”的新组织,未来大组织都在平台上。平台赋能共享服务,个体充分发挥功能,平台最终向生态系统发展,形成自组织的共生、共创、共享的价值体系。第五,社群思维,社群是“自由人的联合体”,已成为继政府和企业后的第三大社会组织，代表数字化时代新的发展方向。

3. The Digital Thinking

The core of digitization is digital thinking, which means the way of digital. There seemed to be five main thoughts actually. Firstly, the data thinking requires fully believe in the power of data. Whoever gets the data gets the world because data trumps logic and the key is the establishment of data values. Secondly, the customer thinking is one of them. Digitization centers on customers and operates customers is the foundation of operation due to the biggest asset of customer community. Consequentially, interacting with customers constantly and serving them endlessly. Thirdly, thinking of link-digitization is all about links, which are greater than ontologies and a mass of links come with lots of resources and chances. Then, realizing online and offline integration totally. Fourthly, thinking of platform-digitization is a platform model, building a new organization of "platform + individual (small group)", and the future large organizations all exist on the platform, where empowers sharing services. Individuals give full ability to their functions and the platform develops into an ecosystem, so as to form a self-organized value system of symbiosis and co-creation. Lastly, thinking of community has become the third largest social organization after the government and enterprises and represents the new development direction of the digital data obviously, which is called "the union of free people".

三、数字之术

The Technology of Digital

数字技术作为数字之术是不断发展的，构成数字技术集群。数字技术是横向技术，对所有纵向的“专业”技术有强大渗透作用，同时赋能专业技术的发展。当今数字技术主要有六大技术，相互协同构成统一体系。

Digital technology is constantly developing fiercely constituting the digital technology cluster. Digital technology is a horizontal technology, which has a strong penetration effect on all vertical "professional" technology and can accelerate its development extremely. It contains six technologies and form a unified system.

1. 大数据技术

大数据为数字化原料。数据是第五生产要素，成为战略性资源。数据对既有生产要素——劳动力、土地、技术和资本起到赋能作用，对四大生产要素产生乘数效应。大数据有很大价值，数据有冷热之分，20%的热数据具有现实价值，单一数据价值有限，多维数据具有使用价值，数据在流动、交互和组合中不断开发其价值。数据产业包括采集、清洗、标注、分析、建模、应用等，数据生态是大产业。

1. Big Data Technology

Digital raw material is big data, which is the fifth factor of production becoming strategic resources. Data not only empower labor, land, technology and capital, but also have multiplier effects on them. There is no denying that big data has great value. Data can be cold or hot and 20% of thermal data process realistic value. While single data has limited value, multidimensional data own utilization value and constantly exploit in flow, interaction and composition. Data industry includes cleaning, annotation, analysis, modeling and application, among which data ecology is a big industry.

2. 人工智能技术

人工智能AI为数字化智能产品。AI是数字技术的核心，已渗透到物理世界的一切领域。AI包括三大部分，即数据、算法和计算，统称为计算力。AI分三大类：计算智能为基本人工智能，能计会算；感知智能为弱人工智能，能看会说；认知智能为强人工智能，能理解会思考。AI为机器学习，机器在人的经验知识基础上，通过数据训练和算法模型产生智能，神经网络使机器自主深度学习。机器学习是向错误学习，在试错过程中对照目标，凡是数据接近目标为“1”，偏离目标为“0”，如此不断迭代优化，从而达成目标。人与机器的关系是协作关系，人始终处于主导地位。

2. Artificial Intelligence Technology

AI belongs to a digital product, which is at the heart of digital technology permeating all areas of the physical world. AI consists of three components-data, algorithms and computation, which is collectively known as computational power. It is divided into three categories such as computational intelligence, perceptual intelligence and cognitive intelligence. Computational intelligence is basic artificial intelligence with numeration ability; What is called weak AI is perceptual intelligence; Cognitive intelligence is the top kind with its ability to understand and think. AI is a kind of machine learning. On the basis of human experience knowledge generates intelligence by the data training and algorithm model on its own initiative. Machine learning is actually from mistakes. In the process of trial and error, It is “1” when the data is close to the target. Nevertheless, when it deviates from the target, it is “0”. The target is achieved through iterative optimization just in this way. Man is always dominate but the relationship between man and machine is cooperative.

3. 云计算技术

云计算为数字化大生产。云分为三大类，有公有云、私有云和混合云。云计算平台有五大功能，分别是云存储、云计算、云应用、云管控和云安全。云平台为大体系，包括专业云计算、分区云计算和边缘云计算等，呈现分布式结构。云平台即服务，服务数据、服务资源、服务软件、服务工具、服务市场等，云平台向智能云计算发展，提供智能解决方案，起到全面赋能作用。

3. Cloud-based Computing

Cloud computing is digital production. Cloud is divided into three categories, namely public cloud, private cloud and hybrid cloud. There are five functions about the cloud computing platform, which are cloud storage, cloud computing, cloud applications cloud management, cloud control and cloud security. Cloud platform is a large system including professional cloud computing, zoned cloud computing and edge cloud computing, presenting a distributed structure. Cloud platform is a service covering service data, resources, software, tools, market and so on, which develops towards intelligent cloud computing and provides solutions with an overall enabling role.

4. 物联网技术

物联网为数字化传输。万物互联构建物联网，数据在物联网上实施互联、互动和互享。物联终端通过传感器产生大量数据在物联网上传输，数据在云平台或边缘平台进行加工计算，再返回物联终端产生智能，“云网端”构建一个体系。物联网有两大关键：一是传感设备，特别是智能传感芯片；二是5G网络，5G能大大加速物联网的发展。

4. Internet of Things Technology

The Internet of Things is digital transmission. Everything is connected to build the Internet of Things, and the data is interconnected, interactive and shared on it. Amount of data are generated through sensors and transmit on IOT terminals. Data is processed and calculated on cloud or edge platform, and then return to IOT terminal to generate intelligence. There are two keys to the Internet of things containing sensor equipment (intelligent sensor chips) and 5G networks, which can greatly accelerate the development of the Internet of Things.

5. 区块链技术

区块链为数字化价值。区块链是数据的记账模式，有公链、私链和联盟链，主要应用于大规模协作网络。区块链是信任链，为机器信任，通过共识机制，实现无中心化自组织。区块链是价值链，通过智能合约，对数据进行确权、流通和交易，实现数据价值和增值。区块链是监管链，通过数据智能实施系统的安全和风险等监管。

5. Blockchain Technology

Blockchain is digital value and a data accounting model with public chains, private chains and consortium chains, which are mainly used in large-scale collaborative networks. Blockchain is a chain of trust, which is trusted by machines and realizes decentralized self-organization through consensus mechanism. Blockchain is a value chain that enable to achieve data value and value-added. It confirms rights, circulates and trades data through smart contracts automatically generated by the system. Blockchain is a chain of supervision that focuses on the security and risk of system through data intelligence.

6. 量子计算技术

量子计算是数字化的升级。量子计算与电子计算相比，速度将提高数万倍，更加高效、更加安全，从更高层次上大大提升人工智能的发展水平。六大数字技术是一个系统工程，它们相互配合，互相赋能，构成数字化的技术体系。

6. Quantum Computing Technology

Quantum computing is the upgrade of digitization, whose speed of quantum computing will be increased by tens of thousands of times compared with electronic computing, which is more efficient and safer and can improve the level of artificial intelligence development from the top-level.

The six digital technology is a system engineering, who cooperate and empower with each other to constitute a digital technology system.

四、数字之用

The Use of Digital

数字化的目的全在于应用，应用之关键是将业务场景、数字技术与专业技术三者融为一体，同时在应用中不断提高数字能力。

The purpose of digitization lies in application and integrates the business scene, digital technology and professional technology, which is the key of it. Continuously improving digital capabilities in applications is an inevitable result.

1. 数字决策

数字化应用的重心是数字决策。经验决策在简单和固定系统是适合的，但在复杂和多变系统里难以适应，这是因为经验的信息量少，信息内容老，而且是主观的局部的认知。数字决策基于大数据分析，数据量大，数据内容及时，而且是客观的真实反映，数字决策适应复杂多变系统，将不确定性化为确定性，从而实现科学决策。

1. Digitization of Decision

The focus of digital application is digital decision

making. The reason why empirical decision making is suitable in simple and fixed systems but not complex and variable one is that the information content of experience is not enough and fresh with subjective and local cognition. Digital decision making is based on big data analysis with the amount of data timely and it is an objective and true reaction that is capable of adapting to complicated and volatile situation. The system turns uncertainty into certainty, enabling scientific decision making.

2.数字化“三生”

所谓数字化“三生”,即数字化生活、数字化生产和数字化生命。数字化生活已十分普及,智能手机就是数字化生活的工具,未来生活每个人都将有一个智能机器人作为智能助理。数字化生产包括智能农业、智能工业、智能服务,通过深化发展,将智能融入各行各业。数字化生命正在加速推进,许多数字器官已经用于人类,特别是人类自身的数字化也在进行,具体路径有人脑与电脑对接、基因数字编辑和数字人。当一个人的所有数据全部上云、上链后,将获得“灵魂永生”。如游戏软件,“第二人生”已升级为“元宇宙”,人生将在数字世界与物理世界一体化“永生”。

2. Digitization “San sheng”

Digitization “San sheng” means digitization life,

digitization production and digitization vita. It has been most popular kind about digitization life, and smart phones are the tools of it. There is an intelligent robot for everyone in the future as an intelligent assistant. Digital production integrates into all industries by deepening development including intelligent agriculture, intelligent industry, intelligent service, etc. Digital vita is accelerating and many digital organs have been used in humans nowadays, especially the digitization of human beings themselves, including the connection between human brain and computer, digital editing of genes, and digital humans. He will receive "soul immortality" after all the data of the person is on the cloud and on the chain. For example, the game software, "Second Life" has been upgraded to a "Meta universe", and life will be integrated into digital world and physical world immortality.

3. 全面数字化

全面数字化为“新四化”，包括经济数字化、社会数字化、城乡数字化和治理数字化。经济数字化其一是数字产业化，即发展数字产业，包括数字硬件业，数字软件业和数字服务业；其二是产业数字化，即各行各业数字化转型，通过产业互联网实现产业智能化发展；在此过程中要突出发展数字基础设施、数字安全和数字货币。新的全球化是数字全球化，发展电子商务和数字贸易。社会数字化是社会生活方方面面的数字化升级，从而建立数字化全新社会。城乡数字化是建设数字城市和数字农村，应用数学技术全面提升城乡发展水平。数字化治理是政府治理的数字化，应用网络平台实现数字政府服务。

3. Comprehensive Digitization

Comprehensive digitization is the new four digitization, including economic digitization, social digitization, urban and rural digitization and governance digitization. First of all, economic digitization is digital industrialization. It contains digital hardware industry, digital software industry and digital service industry. Secondly, the digital transformation of all walks of life achieves industrial development through industrial Internet, which is called industrial digitization. It is necessary to concentrate on the development of digital infrastructure, digital security and digital currency in this process. It is vital to develop e-commerce and digital trade because the new globalization is digital globalization. Social digitization is the digital upgrading of all aspects of social life, so as to establish a new digital society. Urban and rural digitization build digital city and digital rural area, applying mathematical technology to comprehensively improve the level of development there. Digital governance is the digitization of government governance, and realizes digital government services through the application network platform.

4. 数字能力

数字化应用的根本在于数字能力，数字能力已经成为核心能力，以业务能力为基础，数字能力为主导。数字能力是对业务能力的赋能，将产生强大的价值增值效应。决定数字能力有三大关键因素：第一，数据。首先要建立统一的"数字大脑"，如"城市大脑""产业大脑""企业大脑"等，将所有数据包括信息和经验全面汇集，同时将各类系统互联互通，实现大集中、大协同、大共享。第二，人才。从领导、专业人才到员工，都要全力提高"数商"，培训学习数字知识和技能，加快就业结构调整，以适应数字化转型之需。第三，机制。通过数字化改革进行制度创新，特别要鼓励和创造数据自由流动及敢于试错迭代的新机制。

4. Digital Ability

The root of digital application lies in digital ability, which has become the core one. It is based on service capability and led by digital ability. The latter is the empowerment of the former to produce effect of appreciation of value. There are three key factors to decide the digital ability. The first is data, establishing a unified "digital brain" such as "city of brain, "industrial brain" and "enterprise brain" before all data be integrated comprehensively including information and experience. In the meantime, all kinds of systems will be interconnected to achieve greater centralization, coordination and sharing. Besides, talent is also a significant factor. Everyone, from leaders to professionals to employees, should make no efforts to improve "digit quotient" , train and learn digital knowledge skills, and speed up the adjustment of employment structure to meet the needs of digital transformation. The third element is institutional innovation through digital reform. In particular, it is necessary to encourage and create new mechanisms for the free flow of data and the ability to iterate through trial and error.

五、数字之利

The Worth of Digital

数字化创造全新红利，要从人口红利、土地红利转向数据红利，开发数据大金矿，创造数据大价值。

Digitization creates a new dividend and turn the demographic dividend and the land dividend to the data dividend, which generates great value of data.

1. 数字函数公式

数字化的价值体现在相关数学函数公式中：

(1)互联网价值：$V=N^2$，互联网价值与节点总数平方成正比。

(2)产业新价值=(业务能力1+业务能力2+…)×数字能力。

以制造业为例：

新价值=(生产能力+市场能力+研发能力)×数字能力。

1. Digital function formula

The value of digitization is reflected in the relevant mathematical function formula:

(1)Internet value：$V=N^2$，the value of the Internet is proportional to the square of the total number of nodes.

(2) New value ＝ (Service capability 1 ＋ Service capability 2＋…) * digital capability.

Take manufacturing as an example：New value ＝ (Production ability＋ Marketing ability＋ Research and Development ability) * digital ability.

2. 价值增长模型

(1)联合国专家对数字经济的价值增长模型进行了研究，其基本假设是数字经济增长速度为传统经济增长速度的 3.5 倍。当一个系统包括国家、地区、企业的数字化水平超过 75%，在以后不增加投资的基础上，其价值将增长 3 至 5 倍。

(2)IBM 专家对 50 家数字化转型典型企业进行了长达十年的跟踪研究（2007—2017 年），其结论是 50 家企业的销售额平均增长 12 倍，前 3 年增长一倍，后 7 年增长 11 倍。这是因为数据积累有个过程，一旦过了拐点，就会呈现指数级增长。

2. Value-added Model

(1)UN experts have studied the value growth model of the digital economy, which assumes that the digital economy will grow 3.5 times faster than the traditional economy. And its value will increase by 3 to 5 times without additional investment in the future when the digitization level of a system including countries, regions, and enterprises exceeds 75%.

(2) A 10-year-long study about 50 typical enterprise of digital transformation from IBM experts (2007—2017) indicates that sales of the 50 companies increased by an average of 12 times, doubling in the first 3 years and 11 times in the next 7 years because of the process of data accumulation. It grows exponentially once the inflection point is passed.

3. 价值增长机制

数字化的价值增长机制主要得益于两大因素：一是网络协同；二是数据智能。传统企业存在"四不"，即不连接、不匹配、不协同和不及时，严重影响价值创造能力。数字化企业有"四优"，即精准化、高效化、协同化和预判化，通过"四优"克服"四不"就能实现价值倍增，特别是精准和预判，对价值创造能起到决定性的作用。

3. Value Growth Mechanism

Digital value growth mechanism mainly benefits from network collaboration and data intelligence. Traditional enterprises are not connected, matched, coordinated and timely, which seriously affect the value creation ability. Meanwhile, digital enterprises have the "four advantages" of precision, high efficiency, synergy and prediction. It can realize value multiplication through the "four excellent" to overcome the "four no", especially precision and prediction, which play a decisive role in value creation.

4.数字资产

数据不仅是资源,更是资产,也是资本。数字资产不单是数字货币,主要包括数据、软件、知识产权、设计创作、信息网络、微信号、博文等,而且实物资产也可以转化为数字资产。实物资产越用越贬值,而数字资产越用越增值,价值越来越大,未来数字资产将大于实物资产。

4. Digital Assets

Date is not only resources, but also assets and capital. Moreover, Digital assets includes data, software, intellectual property rights, design and creation, information networks, Wechat signals, blogs posts and so on, which are not only digital currency, but also physical assets can be transformed into digital assets. The more physical assets use, the more it depreciates. On the contrary, digital assets grow in value as they are used. As a result, digital assets will be superior to physical assets.

六、总结

Conclusion

数字革命是人类文明历史上最伟大的革命之一，推动经济与社会产生最为深刻的变革。数字化的巨大作用是两大融合，第一，物理世界与数字世界的融合，物理世界为“阳”，数字世界为“阴”，两者成为双胞胎，两大世界的融合使世界更精彩。第二，碳基文明与硅基文明的融合，碳基文明为“生物智能”文明，硅基文明为“机器智能”文明，两者并列双文明，两大文明的融合使世界更美好。数字革命起始于 20 世纪末叶，创造了 21 世纪新时代，到 21 世纪中叶，数字化将进入高级阶段，实现智能大爆发，从更高维度开拓人类文明的全新境界。

The digital revolution is the greatest one in the history of human civilization, which drives the most profound economic and social changes. The great effect of digitization is the integration of two worlds. One is the integration of the physical world（Yang） and the digital world（Yin） contributes the wonderful world, another is the fusion of carbon-based civilization （ biological intelligent civilization） with silicon-based civilization （machine intelligent civilization), which also make a better world. The digital revolution has created a new era in the 21st century, which started at the end of the 20th century and entered an advanced stage in the middle of 21st century. It opens up a new realm of human civilization in a higher dimension and intelligent explosion has been achieved totally.

第二部分　数字经济

Part Two　Digital Economy

一、新经济时代

New Economic Era

(一)新经济大背景

The Background of New Economy

1. 2008 年国际金融危机,带来世界性经济衰退,其本质是全球经济发展的历史性大转折,传统生产方式难以为继,主要出现两大危机:一是资源消耗过大,整个地球每年再生的自然资源增量只能满足全球生产需要资源增量的 2/3,也就是每年地球的自然资源要赤字 1/3。据中国新闻网报道,2016 年全球自然资源增量已全部用完。二是生产能力过剩,全世界整体生产能力的 50% 即可满足全球 73 亿多人口的基本需求,产能大大超过需求。解决这两大危机必须发展新经济。

1. The international financial crisis in 2008 with the essence of a historic turning point in global economic development resulted in a worldwide economic recession. Two crises appear due to the unsustainable traditional mode of production: one is the excessive consumption of

resources; the annual increment of natural resources regenerated by the earth can only meet two-thirds of the increment of global production needs, which means a one-third annual deficit in the earth natural resources. By August 3, 2016, the increment of global natural resources has run out, reported by Chinanews online service. Another crisis is the overcapacity, 50% of the world's overall production capacity can meet the basic needs of more than 7.3 billion people around the world, and production capacity far exceeds demand. It's necessary to develop new economy in order to solve these two major crises.

2. 2015年5月,在中国杭州召开的G20峰会上,各国政要发布《二十国集团数字经济发展与合作倡议》,一致认为数字经济是全球经济增长日益重要的驱动力,将发展数字经济作为未来的主导方向。全球1000强企业领导也认同数字化转型新经济。关于新经济有多种表述,如信息经济、知识经济、网络经济等,但都不能科学表述新经济,因为信息、知识、网络均离不开数字这个基础,数字经济才是最科学的表述,代表新经济的内在逻辑,应定义为数字新经济。发展数字新经济成为全球共识的新战略。

2. At the G20 Summit held in China Hangzhou, May 2015, official leaders from different countries issued the

G20 Digital Economic Development and Cooperation Initiative. They reached consensus that the digital economy is an increasingly important driving force for global economic growth, and the development of digital economy will be the dominant direction in the future. Leaders from the world's top 1000 enterprises also agree with the transformation of digital economy. There are many expressions about new economy, such as information economy, knowledge economy and network economy, etc., however, none of them express new economy scientifically. Due to the inevitable links to digits of information, knowledgc and nctwork, digital economy representing the internal logic of new economy is the most scientific expression, which should be defined as digital new economy. It has become a new strategy of global consensus to develop digital economy.

3. 2016年,数字新经济集中体现在三大标志性事件上:一是2016年8月起全球资本市场市值最高的前五位公司为苹果、谷歌、微软、亚马逊、脸书,皆为数字新经济,全面取代了金融、汽车、石化等传统产业的地位。二是2016年硅谷与华尔街易位,以往是华尔街支撑硅谷的资本需求,现在是硅谷支持华尔街的高科技人才,硅谷的新经济处于主导地位。三是2016年传统产业城市从"锈带"开始走向"智带”，经济已初步复苏，美国汽车城底特律的智能转型即为一例。中国的新四大发明即移动支付、网购、共享单车、高铁，全部应用数字技术，均为数字经济的新发展。

3. The global economy had a new recovery in 2016 when new digital economy has achieved initial success, this mainly embodied on three landmark events: First is that since August 2016, the top five companies with the highest market capitalization in the global capital market are Apple, Google, Microsoft, Amazon and Face book, all of them have applied digital new economy and completely replaced the position of traditional industries such as finance, automobiles and petrochemicals. The second is the trans-location of Silicon Valley and Wall Street in 2016. Wall Street used to support the capital needs of Silicon Valley; however, Silicon Valley has turned to provide high-tech talents for Wall Street and played a dominant role in new economy nowadays. The third is that in 2016, traditional industrial cities began to move from the “rust belt” to “smart belt”, the intelligent transformation of the motor city Detroit embodies initial recovery of economy. The new four inventions in China includes mobile payment, online shopping, shared bikes and railway high-speed, they represent the new

development of digital economy with the application of digital technology.

4. 中国经济改革经历两次大变革。第一次变革，从计划经济走向市场经济；第二次变革，从传统经济走向数字经济。这两次变革都是历史性的伟大变革，现在正处于第二次变革的关键时期。近几年来，发展实体经济引起全球高度重视，但并非传统实体经济，应该是新实体经济。所谓“五新经济”，包括新零售、新制造、新能源、新金融、新交通等，都冠以“新”字，新就新在数字实体经济。所有十大新兴产业都是以数字技术为基因的。如果说 1993 年互联网浪潮是新经济 1.0，2016 年人工智能浪潮则是新经济 2.0。新经济以实体经济为基础，以数字经济为主导，正在重构全球经济新版图，通过提高数字化水平再造未来竞争新优势。

4. China's economic reform has undergone two major changes. The first change turned China from central planning to a market economy, and China is undergoing transformation from traditional economy to digital new economy during the second change. These are historic changes, and we are now at the critical period of the second change. In recent years, the development of real economy, which should be a new real economy but not a traditional one, has attracted worldwide attention. The so-called "five new economies", including new retail, new

manufacturing, new energy, new finance and new transportation sector, etc., they are all attached to the word "new" which means a new application of digital real economy. And all the ten new emerging industries are born of digital economy. If the Internet wave in 1993 represented new economy 1.0, the artificial intelligence wave in 2016 represents new economy 2.0. The new economy based on real economy with digital economy as the leading factor, is reconstructing a new global economic territory and reforging new competitive advantages in the future by improving the level of digitalization.

(二)数字化本质

The Essence of Digitalization

5.世界由物质、能量、信息三大要素组成,物质与能量构成物理世界,信息的数字化构成数字世界。人类正在进行两大迁徙:第一是从互联网的线下向线上迁徙,拓展人类的发展空间;第二是从物理世界向数字世界迁徙,提高人类的发展维度。从物理世界到数字世界是向高维度发展,因为数为高维,代表事物之本质,数学原理为最根本的规则。任何领域一旦引入数学,就会实现认知的精细化,都将从经验走向科学。物理世界解决不了的大量问题,在数学世界得到很好解决,将物理现象转换为数学模型就变得简单易行,物理问题通过数学公式将迎刃而解。最核心的数字就是 0 与 1,大量 0101 的数字集合构成数字世界的一切。

5. The world consists of three elements: material, energy and information. Material and energy compose the physical world, and the digitization of information builds the digital world. Human beings are conducting two grand migrations. The first migration is from offline to online, expanding human's development space. The second is migrating from the physical world to the digital world, improving the development dimension of human beings. Developing from physical world to digital world is a movement to high-dimensional space. The reason is that digits are high-dimensional, representing the essence of

things. As mathematical principles are the fundamental laws. Once Math enters any field, this field would realize the refinement of cognition and cling to science instead of experience. A large number of problems that cannot be solved in the physical world are well solved in the mathematical world. It is simple and practicable to convert physical phenomena into mathematical models and physical problems can be smoothly solved by mathematical formulas. 0 and 1 are core numbers, a great deal of 0101 sets of numbers compose the whole digital world.

6.传统经济建立在实体的基础之上,新经济则建立在数字的基础上,数字新经济改变了基础结构,基本逻辑的变化将改变一切,从根本上变革产业组织方式。从信息化(IT)到数字化(DT)是重大升级,IT 以业务为中心,DT 以数字为中心,从更高维度上发展。新经济作为数字经济,要求构建“数字双胞胎”,就是将实体影射成同样的数字孪生体,形成一实一虚的双胞胎,这是数字经济的根基。

6. While the traditional economy was based on the entity, the new economy is based on digits. Digital new economy has changed the infrastructure, the transformation of basic logic will change everything and reform the way of industrial organization fundamentally. It is a great upgrade to move from Information Technology (IT) to Digital

Technology (DT), while IT centers on business, DT centers on digits and develop in a higher dimension. As digital economy, the new economy need to construct the foundation of digital economy —— "digital twins", that means when the entity is projected into a same digital twinning, a virtual and real twins will be formed.

7.数字经济的本质要求为生产的数字化。数字化生产之关键是实现“两个一切”,即一切业务数字化,一切数字业务化。首先将所有业务转化为数字,通过数字的生产形成数字产品,其次将数字产品返回到业务中去,从而产生新的价值。所有人、物、事都可以数字化,正如人的姓名可有许多重名,而人的身份证号码却是唯一的数字,数字已成为万物之灵魂。

7. The core of the digital economy is to realize the digitalization of production, which means the implementation of "two of all", in terms of the digitization of all business as well as the commercialization of all digits. First, all businesses are converted into digits. Through the production of digits, digital products are formed, then digital products return to the businesses and generate new value. All people, things and events can be digitized. Digit has become the soul of all things just like people may have duplication of names, but they only have one ID number.

(三)网络化联结

Networked Connection

8. 世界本是互联的整体,通过泛在连接形成网络,网络为强大的组织力量,将分散变成集聚。网络具有"三互"机制:一是互联,互联是基础,人、物、信息都可以相互联结,联结越多,资源越多,机会也越多,联结的价值高于主体的价值。二是互动,互动是关键,在互动中产生叠加效应,在交互中形成协同效应。三是共享,共享是目的,通过互联互动实现资源与价值的共享。"三互"成为网络之基因。

8. The world interconnects as a whole, forming a network through ubiquitous connection. Network is a powerful organizational force that will turn decentralization into centralization. The network has a mechanism called "three inters". First is interconnection, interconnection is the foundation. People, things and information can interconnect with each other, the more interconnections there are, the more resources and opportunities there are. The value of interconnection is higher than that of subjects. The second is interaction; interaction is the key which can produce both superposition effect and synergistic effect. The third is sharing; sharing is the purpose, the sharing of resources and value can be achieved through interconnection and interaction. "Three inters" becomes the gene of the network.

9. 网络产生价值，网络的价值由联结而生，联结使价值不断放大，联结的节点越多，价值也越大，当网络中节点一旦突破临界点，就有极其强大的爆发力。网络的价值与节点的平方成正比，呈现价值的指数效应，即网络中有 N 个节点，则其价值为 N^2。如五个点处于分散状态，相加之和再多为 5，互相联结之乘方则为 25。

9. Network produces value, and the value of the network is generated and magnified by connection. The more nodes there are, the greater the value is. Powerful explosive force will appear once the nodes in the network break through the critical point. The value of the network is proportional to the square of the nodes, presenting an exponential effect of value, that is, if there are N nodcs in the network, its value will be N^2. If the five nodes are decentralized and the additive sum is more than 5, the involution of the interconnections will be 25.

10. 新经济以网络为载体，在数字化生产中，数字由网络来传递，用网络来整合，在网络中生产，通过网络实现其价值，特别是互联网，在空间上零距离，在时间上即时化，成为数字化生产的最佳载体。互联网将线下分布式发展转变为线上集聚化发展，成为新经济的最好工具。

10. The new economy takes the network as carrier; digits are transmitted and integrated by the network through the

production. These produced digits can realize their value through the network, especially the Internet, which has become the best carrier due to its zero distance in space and instantaneously on time. The Internet has transformed the distributed development offline into the agglomeration development online, which has become the best tool for new economy.

(四)智能化发展

Intelligent Development

11. 数字新经济的最新发展是全面智能,人类社会从农业文明走向工业文明,现在正走向智能文明。工业革命是人类体力的大解放,智能革命是人类脑力的大解放。走向全面智能是历史发展的必然,人工智能为人类万年文明史上最伟大的变革,人工智能是全面智能的核心。无数不智,没有数字不是智能的,唯有数字方能实现全面智能。

11. The latest development of digital new economy is comprehensive intelligence. Human society is moving from agricultural civilization to industrialcivilization, and is now moving towards intelligent civilization. Thc industrial revolution is the great liberation of human physical strength, and the intellectual revolution is the great liberation of human brain. In the process of history development, it is inevitable to move towards comprehensive intelligence, especially artificial intelligence, which is the greatest change in the history of human civilization. Artificial intelligence is the core of comprehensive intelligence. Without digits, there will be no intelligence; comprehensive intelligence can only be achieved by digits.

12. 人类正在加速走向智能时代,麦肯锡研究院对智能时代与工业时代进行对比研究,基本结论为三大数据:从技术发展速度看,智能时代是工业时代的10倍;从经济规模看,智能时代是工业时代的300倍;从社会影响看,智能时代是工业时代的3000倍;足见智能时代发展的辉煌前景。

12. We are accelerating to a new era of intelligence. McKinsey Research Institute has made a comparison between intelligent age and industrial age; the basic conclusion is three data: the speed of technological development, economic scale and social influence of the intelligent age are respectively 10 times, 300 times and 3000 times than that of the industrial age, this shows the brilliant prospect of intelligent age.

13. 智能时代产生巨大新红利,智能红利具有普惠性,将惠及全体人民,越来越多的富裕人群来自智能新经济。智能红利的核心是大幅度提升经济价值,实现经济价值最大化。智能的价值集中体现在“三化”:一是精准化,产品从0做到90,只能产生50%的价值,从90做到100方能实现最后50%的价值。从90到100的关键在于精准化,智能就是解决精准,智能化使系统获得最优解,特别是决策的最优解。二是定制化,当今客户需求追求个性化定制,智能是解决个性化定制的最优路径,体现客户的最大价值。三是预测化,智能可预测趋势,有利于科学决策;智能可预测问题并自动优化,有利于解决问题。智能全面提升实体经济的高质量发展水平。

13. Intelligent era generates tremendous new dividends. Intelligent dividends are inclusive which will bring benefit to all people. More and more wealthy people come from the new intelligent economy. The core of intelligent dividend is to substantially increase and finally maximize the economic value. The value of intelligence mainly embodies in "three changes": the first is precision, only half of the value can be achieved when producing from 0 to 90, the last ten steps represent another half of the value. The key of moving from 90 to 100 lies in precision. Intelligence helps to solve the problem precisely which can provide optimal solution to systems, especially decisions. The second is customization. Nowadays, the demand of customers pursues personalized customization. Intelligence is the optimal path to solve related issues which can embody the maximum value of customers. The third is prediction, intelligent can predict trends which is conducive to scientific decision-making, at the same time, intelligent can predict problems and optimize them automatically, which is conducive to problem-solving. Intelligence promotes the high-quality development level of the real economy comprehensively.

14.新经济新的衡量标准为 iGDP，i 代表智能化指数，即智能经济占 GDP 的比重，智能经济包括智能产业和智能化应用两个方面，iGDP 超过 50%，标志开始进入智能化新时代。当一个国家、地区、城市或企业智能化水平超过 75%，则在不增加投入的基础上，GDP 达到现有水平的 3.5 倍。智能化的投入产出率高，1 元投入，5 元产出，充分体现智能经济的强大生命力。

14. The new reference point of new economy is iGDP. I represents intellectualize index, which means the proportion of intelligent economy to GDP. Intelligent economy includes two aspects: intelligent industry and intelligent application. When iGDP exceeds 50%, a new era of intellectualize begins. On the basis of maintaining input, when the level of intelligence exceeds 75%, GDP can reach 3.5 times than the current level. The input-output ratio of intelligence is high. For example, if you invest one yuan, you will reap five yuan, this phenomena shows the great vitality of intelligent dividend.

二、数字技术体系

Digital Technology System

(一)数字新技术

Digital New Technology

15.新一轮技术革命的核心是数字技术革命。数字新技术是一个大体系,主要由五大数字技术组成,包括大数据技术、云计算技术、物联网技术、区块链技术、人工智能技术。五大数字技术支撑数字化生产方式,其中大数据为数字资源,云计算为数字平台,物联网为数字传输,区块链为数字信任,人工智能为数字智能,五大新技术相互融合,推动数字新经济快速发展。

15. The core of the new round of technological revolution is the revolution of the digital technology. There is a huge system of digital new technologies consisting of technologies in big data, cloud computing, Internet of things, blockchain and artificial intelligence. The five digital technologies support the digitalized production with

big data as the digital resource, cloud computing as the digital platform, Internet of things as the digital transfer, blockchain as the digital trust and artificial intelligence as the digital intelligence. The five new technologies are integrated so as to boost the rapid development of the digital new economy.

(二)大数据技术

Big Data Technology

16.大数据为数字化生产资源,是21世纪新的战略资源。世界上所有人、事、物、企业、组织每时每刻都在产生大量数据,数据流构成最宝贵的知识财富。数据资源与物质资源相比,数据既不会枯竭,又不会排放废物,可谓取之不尽,用之不竭。一切皆为数据,谁掌握数据,谁就引领未来。中国的人口就是个庞大的数据源,其中五大城市为数据大市:杭州有阿里巴巴;深圳有腾讯、华为;北京有百度、京东、小米;上海有今日头条;贵阳有国家级数据中心。这真所谓"得数据者得天下"。

16. Big data is the resource of the digitalized production and the new strategic resource of the 21st century. Data is being created every moment by every person, event, thing, company and organization. The data flow constitutes the most precious knowledge wealth. Compared to the material resources, data resources will neither be exhausted nor release waste so it can be recognized as an inexhaustible gold mine. Everything is data so who masters data will lead the future. China population is the biggest data resource with five major data cities: Hangzhou with Alibaba, Shenzhen with Tencent and Huawei, Beijing with Baidu, JD. com, Xiaomi, Shanghai with TouTiao and Guiyang as the national data center. It can well be said

that "People who get data get the world".

17. 大数据贵在应用,数据间的相关性具有强大洞察力,广泛用于政府、社会和企业的各个领域。在经济领域,按照功能,大数据主要应用于五大方面:一是数据决策,在数据分析基础上,提供科学决策依据,预测未来发展趋势。二是数据搜索,通过搜索大量社会舆情,特别是网络媒体数据,提供舆情分析发展机会和可能风险。三是数据商务,在大量交易数据和行为数据中,实时提供数据信用、用户需求和精细化管理。四是数据监控,应用数据采集和软件系统,实现实时动态监控管理。五是数据仿真,建立数据虚拟系统,仿真实体运行和模拟结果。

17. The most important of big data is its application. With the strong insight of the relativity, data is widely used in all fields of the government, society and companies. In the field of economy, big data is applied in five aspects according to the functions: first is data decision. Based on the data analysis, scientific decision reasons are provided to forecast the future development trend. Second is data search. Through searching for a big number of public opinions, especially the online media data, pubic opinions are provided to analyze development opportunities and potential risks. Third is data business. Real-time data credit, user demand and specialized management are

provided in business data and behavior data. Fourth is data monitoring. Data collection and software system can be applied to realize real-time dynamic monitoring management. Fifth is data simulation. Data visual system is established to simulate the real operation and outcomes.

(三)云计算技术

Cloud Computing Technology

18.云计算为数字化生产平台,是信息生产方式的重大变革。信息化要从“上网”走向“上云”,实现全面云化,整个社会生产力都要建立在云上。云计算的构成包括基础设施层(lass)、平台层(pass)、软件层(sass)。云为“智慧大脑”,按照分类有:公有云、私有云、混合云和分布云(雾计算)等,可为各类组织提供强大智能,创造全新价值。

18. Cloud computing is a digitalized production platform and a great change in information production. Digitalization should transform from the Internet to the Cloud and a comprehensive cloud cover should be achieved so that the social productivity can be based on the Cloud. Cloud computing consists of lass, pass and sass. Cloud is an "intelligent brain", which can be divided into Public Cloud, Private Cloud, Hybrid Cloud and Distributed Cloud(fog computing). It can provide strong intelligence for various organizations and create new values.

19.云计算的本质是服务,根据云计算功能主要提供五大服务:一是云空间,云计算的硬件是服务器,租用服务器空间,提供云平台基础服务。二是云存储,云上存储大量公共数据,也为用户存储专用数据，成为数据服务的大平台。三是云计算，云上有大规模高效率的计算设备，为用户提供强大的计算能力服务。四是云应用，云计算的核心是软件系统的应用服务，各类模块包括内容服务、专业服务和定制服务专家系统等。五是云安全，云计算对于安全有足够的技术大保障，确保用户数据安全。

19. The essence of cloud computing is service. According to the functions, cloud computing provides mainly the following five services: first is cloud space. The hardware of cloud computing is the server. Server space is usually rented to provide basic service for the cloud platform. Second is cloud storage. Both public data and individual data are stored on cloud so it serves as a big platform for data service. Third is cloud computing. A large scale of efficient computing devices is equipped on cloud to provide strong computing service for users. Fourth is cloud application. The core of cloud computing is application service of the software system which consists of content service, professional service and specialized service expert system. Fifth is cloud security. Cloud computing provides technological safeguard for security to ensure the security of users' data.

(四)物联网技术

Internet of Things Technology

20. 物联网为数字化生产传输。互联网的发展历程,从普通互联网到移动互联网再到物联网,实现信息的互联、人的互联、物的互联,万物互联产生重大经济与社会价值。物联网的本质是传输,即数据传输服务。物联网的组成主要包括感知层、网络层和应用层,由此构建物联网的架构体系。随着5G通信和量子通信的发展,传输速度将大大加快,使物联网的发展突飞猛进。

20. Internet of things is digitalized production transfer. Internet of things has developed from the ordinary Internet to mobile Internet and finally to Internet of things, and achieved interconnectivity among information, people and things. Great interconnectivity in everything has created rich economic and social values. The essence of Internet of things is transfer, namely, data transfer service. Internet of things mainly consists of perception layer, network layer and application layer, which constitute the architecture of Internet of things. With the development of 5G communication and quantum communication, the transfer speed will be raised to a much higher level so that Internet of things will achieve a rapid development.

21. 物联网的应用十分广泛,几乎涵盖经济、社会和民生等方面。

其应用功能集中体现在四个方面：一是数据识别，采用传感器和射频设备等感知技术，随时随地识别并获得海量数据。二是动态监测，物联网采集的大量数据，可用于对事物的动态监测。三是定位跟踪，通过对事物的定位系统 GPS 等进行动态跟踪，达到对目标的远程监控。四是智能控制，每个实体都可成为智能终端，手机是最普通的智能终端，汽车是最大的智能终端，特别是 VR、AR、MR 等可穿戴设备，可大大增强应用体验，实现智能控制。

21. Internet of things has a wide range of applications, covering almost all the aspects in economy, society and people's lives. Its applications are mainly demonstrated in the four aspects: first is data identification. Sensing technologies such as sensors and RF devices can be used to identify and obtain massive amounts of data anytime and anywhere. Second is dynamic monitoring. The massive amounts of data collected by Internet of things can be used in dynamic monitoring. Third is location tracking. Through the dynamic tracking of the positioning system GPS, remote monitoring of the target is achieved. Fourth is smart control. Each entity can become a smart terminal, in which, the mobile phone is the most common one amd the car is the largest one. It should be noted that wearable devices such as VR, AR, MR can greatly cnhance the application experience and realize smart control.

(五)区块链技术

Blockchain Technology

22. 区块链为数字化生产信任,旨在解决对数据的信任管理。区块链具有两大功能:一是机器信任,通过分布式数据存储,改变第三方存储,实现机器自我数据管理。二是智能合约,采取点对点加密和共识机制,改变传统协议,达到"不造假、不篡改、可追溯"的可信性,实施零信任成本。区块链引领信息互联网走向价值互联网,将"人、物、事、时、空"五大要素连接一体,通过机器信任和智能合约构建价值传递的大型合作网络。

22. Blockchain is digitalized production trust and aims to deliver trust management of data. Blockchain has two major functions: first is machine trust. Distributed data storage changes the third-party storage method and achieves machine-self data management. Second is the smart contract. An point-to-point encryption and consensus mechanism is adopted to change the traditional agreement, achieve the credibility of "no fraud, no tampering, traceability" and implement zero trust cost. Blockchain leads Internet of information to Internet of values and combines the five major elements of "people, things, events, time and space" to build a big cooperation network for value transfer through machine trust and the smart contract.

23. 区块链的思维原理具有普遍性价值，区块链技术最先应用于数字货币，如比特币等，但不是其全部应用。最主流的应用是在产业上，区块链成功应用于金融、物联网、供应链、能源、交通、制造、医疗、公益及公共服务等，随着技术的发展，区块链将在众多领域普及应用。区块链重构商业模式、改善用户体验、优化业务流程、实现资源共享、降低交易成本、改变定价规则、提高协同效率，产生极有价值的产品。区块链通过通证技术将数字资产证券化，其财富效应多倍于房地产，发展前景无限广阔。

23. The theory of blockchain has universal values, and the blockchain technology is first applied to digital currencies, such as bitcoin, and many other applications. The mainstream application is in the industries. The blockchain has been successfully applied in finance, Internet of things, supply chain, energy, transportation, manufacturing, medicine, welfare and public services. With the development of technologies, the blockchain will be universally applied in many fields. The blockchain rebuild the business models, improve user experience, optimize business process, achieve resources sharing, reduce transaction cost, change pricing rules, raise coordination efficiency and produce valuable products. The blockchain securitizes digital assets through the token technology, and its wealth effect is 10 times that of real estate. Apparently, it enjoys indefinite development prospect.

(六)人工智能技术

Artificial Intelligence Technology

24. 人工智能为数字化生产智能,是智能化发展的最高阶段,也是生产力发展的最新成果,对经济和社会产生巨大影响,推动人类走向更高智慧。人工智能的本质是机器革命,第一次机器革命是蒸汽机,解放人的体力,成为"劳动的机器"。第二次机器革命是人工智能,解放人的脑力,成为"思考的机器",人工智能作为智能机器将不断自我进化,人工智能融合一切,前景无可估量又无法预测。

24. Artificial intelligence is digitalized production intelligence, the highest level of intelligentization and the newest fruit of the development of productivity. It has great impact on economy and society, advancing human beings to higher intelligence. The essence of artificial intelligence is machine revolution. The first machine revolution gave birth to the steam, which emancipated human labor so as to become a "labor machine". The second machine revolution resulted in artificial intelligence which emancipated humans' brains so as to become a "thinking machine". As an intelligent machine, artificial intelligence will keep advanced and integrate everything so that in the future, will be unpredictable and incredible.

25. 人工智能由三大要素构成：一是数据，海量数据为人工智能的基础，人工智能不吃大米专吃数据。二是算法，科学算法为人工智能的核心，算法是将数学模型求解，算法决定人工智能的水平。三是计算，计算资源为人工智能的关键，强大的计算能力支撑人工智能的运营。数据、算法和计算三者是个整体，其基本流程是先把业务问题转化为数学模型（列方程），由算法来求解模型（解方程），将算法编成软件（复制），用数据运算软件（结果）。人工智能的工作机制是机器学习，机器根据初始条件和工作目标，运用数据反复学习，在学习中不断反馈试错和迭代优化，最后达成目标。机器学习可以根据人的经验学习，也可以不需要人的经验自我学习，由机器与环境的不断互动或者两个人工智能系统的对抗性竞争，赋予机器从未企及的智能想象力。通过深度学习和群体学习的机器，越来越聪明，越来越优秀，最先进的是人工智能加量子计算，将成为人工智能的全新发展。

25. Artificial intelligence is composed of three major elements: first is data. Massive amounts of data lay a foundation for artificial intelligence. It can be said that artificial intelligence does not eat rice but data. Second is algorithm. Scientific algorithm is the core of artificial intelligence. Algorithm a resolve to the mathematical model and it decides the quality of artificial intelligence. Third is calculation. Calculation resources are the key to artificial intelligence. Strong calculation abilities support

the operation of artificial intelligence. Data, algorithm and calculation are a whole. The basic process is first to transform the business issue to a mathematical model (formulate an equation), find the resolve to the model (solve the equation), write the algorithm into a software (copy) and operate the software with data (result). The working mechanism of artificial intelligence is machine learning. According to the initial conditions and work objectives, the machine uses data to learn repeatedly, and continuously feedbacks trial errors and optimizes iteratively in the process of learning, and finally achieves the goal. Machine learning can be based on people's experience, or it can be self-learning without human experience. The constant interaction between machines and the environment or the confrontational competition of two artificial intelligence systems gives the machine an intelligent imagination that has never been achieved. Machines after deep learning and group learning become more and more intelligent, more and more excellent. The most advanced is artificial intelligence plus quantum computing, which will become a new development of artificial intelligence.

26. 人工智能根据功能分为三大类：一是计算智能，代替人工计算，会存储能计算。二是感知智能，模仿感觉器官，会听会看能说话。三是认知智能，模拟神经网络，会分析能思考。人工智能是不断发展的，从弱人工智能到强人工智能，再到超人工智能。弱人工智能是单功能的智能，强人工智能是系统化的智能，超人工智能是群体智能。人工智能能否全面超越人类，关键在于人类的自觉控制。

26. Artificial intelligence is divided into three categories according to the functions: first is computational intelligence. Replacing manual calculation, it does well in storage and calculation. Second is perception intelligence. It can imitate the sensory organs to listen, see and speak. Third is cognitive intelligence. It simulates neural networks to analyze and think. Artificial intelligence is constantly evolving, from weak artificial intelligence to strong artificial intelligence then to super artificial intelligence. Weak artificial intelligence is a single-function intelligence while strong artificial intelligence is a systematic intelligence, and super artificial intelligence is a group intelligence. Whether artificial intelligence can completely surpass human beings lies in the conscious control of human beings.

27. 人与人工智能的关系十分重要，人工智能与人不是对立的，而是互补的，无人化并不是人工智能的目的。人工智能虽然导致部分工作岗位消失，但也会产生新的工作岗位，更可喜的是缩短人们的工作时间，以往是人为机器服务，现在是机器为人服务。人与机器是合作关系，集中体现在两个方面：第一人与机器的融合，机器从事作业，人掌握数据，从采集数据、阅读数据到使用数据，将劳务员工转化为数字员工，成为“新员”人才。第二人脑与电脑的融合，即人工智能与人类智能的结合，“AI＋HI”将是全新的工作机制，实现人与机器的和谐发展。

27. The relationship between human and artificial intelligence is very important. Artificial intelligence is not opposite but complementary to people. Unmanned function is not the purpose of artificial intelligence. Although artificial intelligence has caused some jobs to disappear, it will also create new jobs. What is more gratifying is to shorten people's working time. In the past, people served the machines, but now machines serve the people. The relationship between men and machines is mainly demonstrated in two aspects: first is the integration of men and machines. Machines are engaged in work and people master the data the process of collecting data, reading data to using data transforms the labor into

digital employees as “new staff”. Second is the integration of human brains and computers, namely, the integration of artificial intelligence and human intelligence. “AI+HI” will be a new working mechanism to achieve harmonious development of human and machines.

三、新经济模式

New Economic Model

(一)经济组织模式

Economic Organization Model

28. 新经济是新模式经济，模式不断创新、层出不穷，主要的新模式包括用户经济、平台经济、共享经济、服务经济和价值经济等。这五大新模式相互结合，又产生众多新业态，创造大量新物种，呈现爆发式增长的发展态势，充分体现新经济发展的多样化，激发新经济发展的新动能。

28. The new economy is a new model economy, and the model is constantly innovating and emerging. The main new models such as user economy, platform economy, sharing economy, service economy and value economy are combined so as to create many new business models and new species. It is showing a development trend of explosive growth, fully reflects the diversification of new economic development and stimulates new growth drivers

of new economic development.

(二)用户经济

User Economy

29.新经济最鲜明的特征是以用户为中心,这是因为数字反映用户的本质需求,能为用户画像。互联网拥有空间上零距离、时间上即时化,离用户最近等特点。传统经济以企业为本位,一切从企业自身出发,据专家统计传统企业100件事情中,有85%的事情为企业,只有15%的事情为用户。新经济以用户为本位,一切围绕用户出发,将用户的需求放在首位。企业从B2C转向C2B是根本性大转变,C2B是新经济最大的战略定位,始终为用户创造价值,将用户价值最大化作为企业的根本目标。

29. The most striking feature of the new economy is centering around users. It's because the numbers reflect the users' essential needs and can be used as portray. The Internet is the closest to users because it bears no distance in space and it's instant in real time. The traditional economy is based on the enterprise. Everything starts from the enterprise itself. According to experts, among 100 things in the traditional enterprise, 85% are for the enterprises while only 15% are for the users. The new economy is user-oriented, and everything starts from the users, putting the users' needs first. The shift from B2C to

C2B is a fundamental big change. C2B is the biggest strategic positioning of the new economy. It always creates value for users and sets the maximization of user values as the fundamental goal of the company.

30.以用户为主导,重点要做好三件事情:一是用户定位,明确企业的用户群,精心组织具有相同价值观的用户,特别要重视服务好20%的"黄金客户"。二是用户互动,强化用户体验,突出用户沟通,充分了解用户的"痛点",解决用户的核心需求。三是用户参与,用户参与企业经营,从产品设计、使用、定价、营销等环节全方位参与,解决用户个性化定制需求。用户主导并不是简单地满足需求,而是在相互迭代中引领需求,与用户共创价值,与用户共同成长。

30. Focus should be put on three things to achieve user-oriented: first is user positioning. The user group of enterprises should be made clear and users of the same values should be organized. Special attention should be paid to the 20% "golden customers". Second is user interaction. It is important to improve user experience, emphasize user communication and understand the users' demands so as to meet the core needs of the users. Third is user participation. Users fully participate in business operations, from product design, use, pricing and marketing to meet the users' personalized customization

needs. User-led is not simply to meet the demand, but to lead the demand in mutual iteration, create values with the users, and develop with the users.

31. 从经营产品走向经营用户，用户身上有张价值网，拥有巨大的需求，关键要从产品思维上升到用户思维，围绕用户价值网进行经营。经营产品是入口，交易仅是用户价值的开端，挖掘用户潜在价值才是目的。传统经营是规模经济的产品思维，将 1 个产品（服务）卖给 100 个人，新经济是范围经济的用户思维，将 100 个产品（服务）卖给 1 个人。交易仅完成一半业务，另一半是人的数据，经营好人是经营的根本。

31. From operating products to operating users, users have a value network with huge demand. The key is to rise from product thinking to user thinking, and operate around the user value network. Operating products is the entrance, and trading is only the beginning of user values. The purpose is to tap the potential values of the users. Traditional management is a product thinking of economies of scale, selling one product to 100 persons. The new economy is a user thinking of economies of scope, selling 100 products (services) to one person. The transaction only completes half of the business, the other half is the person's data. The good operation of people lays a foundation for the whole operation.

(三)平台经济

Platform Economy

32.平台经济是新经济最重要的组织形式。纵观企业发展,总体上企业分为两大类型:一类为专业公司;一类为平台公司。两类公司各具特色,共同发展。全球100大公司中70%为平台公司,其价值占总量80%多。2016年12月,全球十大平台经济体的市值已经超过十大工业经济体的市值。平台经济可分为企业平台、行业平台、生态平台三大类。平台公司是联合舰队,其竞争力远远超过航空母舰的大公司,具有规模性和灵活性的双重优势。

32. The platform economy is the most important organization form of the new economy. Throughout the development of enterprises, they can be generally divided into two types, one is professional companies, the other is platform companies. The two types of companies have their own characteristics but develop together. 70% of the world's top 100 companies are platform companies, whose values account for more than 80% of the total. In December 2016, the market value of the world's top ten platform economies has exceeded the market value of the top ten industrial economies. The platform economies can be divided into three categories: enterprise platform, industry platform and ecological platform. The platform company is a joint fleet, and its competitiveness far

exceeds that of a large company of aircraft carriers, with the dual advantages of scale and flexibility.

33.企业平台的核心是供应链管理平台，每个企业都有供应链，特别是大企业的供应链环节多、链条长、规模大。供应链管理存在诸多问题，主要是效率低、协同差、应变慢，构建供应链平台应运而生。企业供应链平台要集中解决两大问题：一是供应链成员诚信，重点是质量、价格和交货期等诚信保证；二是供应链成员协同，平台建立高效服务流程，大幅度减少库存，提高对用户的应变能力，确保供应链整体协同。

33. The core of the enterprise platform is the supply chain management platform. Each enterprise has a supply chain. In particular, large enterprises have many supply chain links, long chains and large scales. There are many problems in supply chain management, mainly low efficiency, poor coordination, and slow response. The construction of supply chain platform came into being. The enterprise supply chain platform should focus on solving two major problems: first, the integrity of the supply chain members, with emphasis on quality, price and delivery time; and second, the collaboration of supply chain members. The platform establishes efficient service processes, greatly reduces inventory and improves

resilience to users so as to ensure the overall synergy of the supply chain.

34. 行业平台要从做企业上升到做产业，立足点放在整个产业，以产业发展为己任。行业平台的宗旨是服务：一是服务对象，为整个产业中的供应方、需求方、合作方、支持方等。二是服务内容，产业基本服务和专业服务，产供销等基本服务和公共服务由平台提供，众多专业服务由第三方专业公司提供，特别是金融服务为行业平台最高端的专业服务。三是开源服务，由平台向社会开放，包括数据库、共用硬件（工具）、基础软件等，吸收大量开发者和创客到平台创新开发。行业平台的商业模式为 S2B2C，即 S 为平台提供服务，B 为专业公司或团队进行运作，C 为用户或者消费者。

34. The industry platform should be raised from doing business to doing industry, based on the whole industry and taking industry development as its own responsibility. The purpose of the industry platform is to serve: first, the service target is the supplier, demander, partner, and supporter in the entire industry. Second, service content is basic services and professional services. Basic services such as production, supply and marketing, and public services are provided by the platform. Many professional services are provided by third-party professional companies. It should be noted that financial services are the highest-end

professional services of the industry platform. Third is open source for services, which are open to the public by the platform, including databases, shared hardware (tools), and basic software. They attract a large number of developers and makers to the platform for innovative development. The business model of the industry platform is S2B2C, that is, S provides services for the platform, B operates for professional companies or teams, and C is users or consumers.

35. 生态平台是平台的高级形态，产业间的最终竞争是生态系统的竞争，生态平台由跨界发展组成产业生态系统。产业生态平台具有诸多优势：一是共生优势，大量要素集合产生共生效应；二是协同优势，不同要素融合生成新的物种；三是进化优势，生态系统为自组织，通过交互迭代实现自我进化。

35. The ecological platform is the advanced form of the platform. The final competition among the industries is the competition of the ecosystem. The ecological platform constitutes the industrial ecosystem through cross-border development. The industrial ecological platform has many advantages: first, the symbiotic advantage. A large number of elements gather to produce a symbiotic effect. Second is synergy. Different elements are integrated to

generate new species. Third is the evolutionary advantage. The ecosystem is self-organized, and achieves self-evolution through interactive iteration.

36. 平台的根本在于运营,在平台发展中运营起到决定性作用。运营好平台要强化三大能力,一是信息化能力,平台的载体是信息网络。平台中各种要素和成员都要由网络相互连接,通过数据高效驱动业务,从互联网平台进而向云服务平台发展。二是资源整合能力,平台的关键在于整合资源。平台自身要有核心资源,然后整合社会资源,提高平台的服务规模和能力。三是协同管理能力,平台必须制定各种标准和规范,加强公共管理。对平台上所有成员,一方面进行赋能;另一方面组织监控,使整个平台系统高效发展。平台要实现多前端、强后台、广生态的大格局。

36. The foundamental of the platform lies in its operation, which plays a decisive role in the development of the platform. To operate a good platform, it is necessary to strengthen three major capabilities: first, the informationization capability. The carrier of the platform is the information network. The various elements and members of the platform must be connected by the network to drive the business efficiently through data so that it will develop from the Internet platform to the cloud service platform. Second, the resource integration

capability. The key to the platform is to integrate resources. The platform itself must have core resources, and then integrate social resources to improve the scale and capabilities of the platform. Third, the collaborative management capability. The platform must formulate various standards and norms and strengthen public management. For all members of the platform, on one hand, empowerment should be carried out, on the other hand, it is necessary to organize monitoring so that the entire platform system will develop efficiently. The platform must achieve a large landscape of multiple frontiers, strong backup, and a wide ecology.

(四)共享经济

Sharing Economy

37."共享"是新的经济形态,共享经济是资源革命,改变人们对资源的占有和使用方式,从资源的占有为主走向资源的使用为主,今后人们占有的资源越来越少,而使用的资源则越来越多。共享经济标志人类进入"人人时代",面对资源人人都可以参与,每个人既是生产者,又是供应者,也是消费者,在共享的平台上形成"人人经济"的新模式。

37. "Sharing" is a new economic form. The sharing economy is a resource revolution that changes people's

possession and use of resources from mainly possession to mainly use. People can reach fewer and fewer resources in the future while the resources used are more and more. Sharing economy marks that human beings enter the "everyone era", and everyone can participate in resources. Everyone is a producer, a supplier, and a consumer, forming a new model of "everyone's economy" on a shared platform.

38.共享经济的发展领域极其广泛，基本可分为三大类：一为生活共享，在交通出行、住宿空间、美食分享、医疗健康等场景已取得明显成效；二为生产共享，在生产设备、办公场所、金融需求、通信能源、生产能力服务等领域也有较好应用；三为知识共享，在知识学习、文化教学、内容服务等方面也开始进入。随着时代的发展，共享经济将越来越宽广，在整个经济中的占比大幅度提升，对经济的贡献也越来越大。

38. The development of the sharing economy is extremely broad and can be divided into three major categories: one is life sharing, and has achieved remarkable results in transportation, accommodation, food sharing, and medical health. Second, production sharing. It also has good applications in production equipment, office space, financial needs, communication energy, production capacity services and other fields. Third, knowledge

sharing. It has also begun to enter in knowledge learning, cultural teaching, and content services. With the development of the times, the sharing economy will become wider and wider, the proportion in the entire economy will be greatly increased, and the contribution to the economy will be greater and greater.

39. 共享经济的基本要素包括平台、资源、公众和收入，在同一生态系统中实现共享。平台是共享经济的强大后台，主要负责资源组织和运营管理。平台建立在信息网络基础上，大体有四种模式：一是C2C模式，个人对个人，为自由市场的回归；二是C2B模式，个人对企业，众包和众筹成为新的潮流；三是B2C模式，企业对个人，以租代售的新型生态；四是B2B模式，企业对企业，从消费到生态的共享。随着共享经济的不断发展，共享平台走向智能云服务是大势所趋。

39. The basic elements of the sharing economy include platforms, resources, the public and income, sharing in the same ecosystem. The platform is a powerful background for the sharing economy, and is mainly responsible for resource organization and operation management. The platform is based on the information network, and there are basically four modes: first, the C2C model, Customer-to-Customer, which is a return to the free market. Second, the C2B model, Customer-to-

Business, in which crowdsourcing and crowdfunding has become a new trend. Third, the B2C model, Business-to-Customer, a new type with renting replacing selling. Fourth, the B2B model, Business-to-Business, sharing from consumption to ecology. With the continuous development of the sharing economy, it is an irresistible trend for sharing platforms to move toward intelligent cloud services.

(五)服务经济

Service Economy

40.新经济以大服务为主线,服务经济是大经济,农业、工业、服务业等都需要服务,经济走向全面服务化。对于服务经济我们应有新的认知:一是服务与业务的关系,服务与业务分属不同层次,业务属于作业层面,农业、工业、服务业都有自身的作业,统称为业务。服务属于指导层面,服务指导业务,比业务的层面更高。二是服务的主体价值,业务创造基础价值,随着经济的服务化,价值链的中心发生转移,服务处于中心地位,创造主体价值,关键在于提高深度服务的能力。

40. The new economy is dominated by large services. The service economy is a big economy. The agricultural, industrial, and service industries all need services so the economy is moving towards fully serviced. There should be a new understanding of the service economy: first, the

relationship between service and business, service and business belong to different levels. Business belongs to the operation level, and the agricultural, industrial, and service industries all have their own operations, collectively referred to as business. Service belongs to the guiding level, and service guides the business, which means it is higher than the business level. Second, the main value of the service. The business creates the basic value. With the service of the economy, the center of the value chain shifts, in which the service is at the center so as to create the main values. The key is to improve the ability of deep service.

41.产业服务是服务经济的重心，服务贯穿于产业的全过程，产业的业务前、业务中、业务后都需要服务。以制造业为例，科技研发、设计开发、物资供应、物流仓储、生产运维、商品营销、金融投资等都为生产性服务，服务支撑了生产制造，提升制造业的发展水平，服务创造价值将与日俱增。

41. Industrial service is the focus of the service economy. Service runs through the whole process of the industries. The industries needs services before, during and after business. Taking manufacturing as an example, technology research and development, design and development,

material supply, logistics and warehousing, production and operation, commodity marketing, and financial investment are all productive services. Service supports production and manufacturing, enhances the development level of manufacturing, and creates values for services with each passing day.

42. 企业服务是新兴服务产业。传统生产性服务内置在制造企业内部,成为附属性服务。现代生产性服务从中分离出来,成为第三方专业公司,形成独立的企业服务产业。专业服务公司由于具有专业程度高、服务规模大、成本相对低、质量水平高等诸多优势,为全社会提供专业化服务体系和整体解决方案,对提升主体企业发展水平发挥决定性作用。

42. Enterprise services are emerging service industries. Traditional production services are built into manufacturing companies and become affiliated services. Modern productive services are separated and become third-party professional companies, forming an independent enterprise service industry. Due to its high degree of professionalism, large scale of service, relatively low cost and high quality, professional service companies provide professional service systems and overall solutions for the whole society, which plays a decisive role in improving the development level of the

main enterprises.

43.新服务形态不断涌现,传统经营方式是卖产品送服务。新经营方式是送产品卖服务,将产品作为载体送给用户,通过卖服务来获取回报。卖产品只能卖一次,而卖服务可以持续卖下去,只要产品在使用,服务是永续的,可获取源源不断的现金流,卖服务的价值远远超过卖产品的价值。正如洗衣机和洗衣的关系,卖洗衣机产品只赚一次钱,用洗衣机为人们洗衣服务可以不断赚钱,这种全新的服务经营方式是大有可为的。

43. The new service forms are constantly emerging. The traditional way of doing business is to sell products and present services. The new way of doing business is to present products and sell services, to present products as carriers to users, and to obtain returns by selling services. Selling products can only be once, but selling services can be constant. As long as the products are in use, the service is sustainable, and a steady stream of cash can be obtained. The value of selling services far exceeds the value of selling products. Just like the relationship between washing machines and laundry, selling washing machines only earns one time while providing laundry services with washing machines can make money constantly. This new service operation method is promising.

(六)价值经济

Value Economy

44.企业经营的目的是创造价值,新经济以价值至上。价值经济要处理好两大关系:一是价值与价格之间关系,价格是价值的体现,创造价值为根本,不要习惯于在价格上做减法,重要的是在价值上做加法。二是价值与利润之间的关系,利润是实现价值的结果,价值始终高于利润,企业应以价值至上。现在有两类企业:一类是赚钱企业;另一类是值钱企业。值钱企业是高价值企业,拥有强大的用户资源、数据资源和现金流,近期可能利润不高,而长期产生的利润将持续上升。

44. The purpose of business management is to create values, and the new economy pays the highest premium to values. Value economy must deal with two major relationships: first, the relationship between value and price. Price is the embodiment of value. Creating value is the fundamental. It shouldn't be used to doing subtraction on price while it is important to add values. Second is the relationship between value and profit. Profit is the result of realizing value. Value is always higher than profit. Enterprises should take value first. There are now two types of enterprises, one is profitable enterprises and the other is valuable enterprises. Valuable enterprises are high-value companies with strong user resources, data

resources and cash flow. In the near term, profits may not be high but the long-term profits will continue to rise.

45. 企业价值的衡量，对于上市公司来说是市值，对于未上市公司来说是估值，两者都是市场对企业价值的客观评价，为最真实的企业价值。评价市值的指标较多，如营业额、利润、资产等，但最为核心的是现金流，市值是对未来现金流的时间贴现值，体现企业发展能力，企业价值要以自由现金流为主，以长期发展为至上。

45. The measurement of corporate value is the market value for listed companies and the valuation for unlisted companies. Both are objective evaluations of the corporate value by the market and the most real value. There are many indicators for evaluating market value, such as turnover, profit and assets, but the core is cash flow. The market value is the time discounted value of future cash flow, reflecting the development capability of the enterprise. The value of the enterprise should be based on free cash flow, with long-term development as the supremacy.

46. 结构为事物本质之体现，价值结构与业务结构是倒置的。企业的业务结构为正三角，底层是基本业务，中层是增值业务，上层是定制业务。而其价值结构为倒三角，底层价值最小，中层价值次之，上层价值最大。为此提升企业价值要在基本业务基础上，多做增值业务，进而向定制业务发展。

46. Structure is the embodiment of the essence of things, value structure and business structure are inverted. The business structure of the enterprise is a triangle. The bottom layer is the basic business, the middle layer is the value-added service, and the upper layer is the specialized business. The value structure is an inverted triangle. The bottom layer value is the smallest, the middle layer value is the second, and the upper layer value is the largest. To enhance the value of the enterprise, more value-added services on the basis of basic business should be taken to develop a customized business.

47. 价值经济新的商业模式是一体两翼，即以实体企业为中心，在实体基础上增加两翼，一翼为科技，新科技为企业价值倍增；一翼为资本，产业金融和资本运作为企业价值升值。资本与科技相结合将产生巨大的价值。企业实体固然重要，但仅在地上只能爬行，增加两翼方能飞行，一体两翼的商业模式是提升企业价值的腾飞之路。

47. The new business model of value economy is one body with two wings, that is, focusing on the entity enterprise, adding two wings on the entity basis, among which, one is technology, new technology is multiplying the value of the

enterprise; the other is capital, industrial finance and capital operation enjoy appreciation as corporate values. The combination of capital and technology will generate tremendous value. Corporate entities are important indeed, but they can only crawl on the ground. Only with the two wings can they fly. The business model of one body with two wings is the way to enhance the value of the enterprise.

四、智能大生态

Smart Ecology

(一)智能生态体系

Smart Ecological System

48. 智能化为大生态体系，对于一个地区、一个城市来说，智能化建设需要形成智能生态体系。这个体系的结构由三大部分构成，即一个核心、两大支柱。一个核心是智能数字大脑；两个支柱是智能产业化和产业智能化。在整个体系中，所有节点交互融合、相互协同，实现动态进化发展。

48. Intellectualization is a large ecosystem. For a region and a city, intellectualization construction requires the formation of an intelligent ecosystem. The structure of this system consists of three major components, namely, one core and two pillars. The core is the intelligent digital brain, and the two pillars are intelligent industrialization and industrial intellectualization. Throughout the system,

all junctures interact and collaborate to achieve dynamic evolution.

(二)智能数字大脑

Intelligent Digital Brain

49.智能数字大脑是整个生态体系的核心,起到总体组织作用。智能数字大脑由三大部分组成:一是大数据中心,将海量数据集中建立数据库,实现数据共享;二是基础软件系统,将大量基础软件系统模块化,实现开源的公共服务;三是智能云平台,建立智能化云平台,强化网络安全,为全社会提供可靠的智能服务。

49. The intelligent digital brain is at the heart of the entire ecosystem, playing an overall organizational role. The intelligent digital brain consists of three major parts: first, the big data center, which builds a database of massive data to achieve data sharing. Second, the basic software system, which modularizes a large number of basic software systems and implements source-open public services. Third, the intelligent cloud platform. An intellectualized cloud platform is built to strengthen network security, and provide reliable intelligent services for the whole society.

(三)智能产业化

Intelligent Industrialization

50.智能化的基础是智能产业化,智能产业发展快、规模大、品类多。首先是智能硬件,在产业群中有智能芯片、智能传感设备、智能显示设备、智能装备、智能终端、可穿戴产品、虚拟现实、机器人、无人机等,每一方面都是一个大产业。智能硬件作为智能产业的设施,其应用十分宽广。

50. The basis of intellectualization is intelligent industrialization. The intelligent industry is developing rapidly with many categories at a large scale. The first is intelligent hardware. In the industrial cluster, there are smart chips, smart sensing devices, intelligent display devices, smart devices, smart terminals, wearable products, virtual reality, robots, drones, etc., each of which is a big industry. As a smart industry facility, intelligent hardware is widely used.

51.软件定义一切,与智能硬件相比,智能软件尤为重要。智能软件产业群中有智能系统软件、智能专业软件、智能应用软件、众多嵌入式软件、大量APP、小程序、二维码等。智能软件与硬件相结合并不断升级,将提供各种场景的智能系统和整体解决方案。软件已成为核心能力,企业应用软件的规模与水平将决定未来的竞争能力。

51. Software defines everything, and intelligent software

is especially important compared to smart hardware. The intelligent software industry cluster includes intelligent system software, intelligent professional software, intelligent application software, numerous embedded software, a large number of APPs, small programs, and QR codes. Intelligent software and hardware are combined and continuously upgraded to provide intelligent systems and overall solutions to a variety of situations. Software has become a core competency, and the scale and level of the enterprise applications will determine its future competitiveness.

52.增材制造即3D打印,为新型智能产业,是生产制造方式的重大变革,对实现产品智能化,加快研究设计、降低材料消耗、提高工作效率起到难以估量的作用。3D打印广泛用于新品设计、模具开发、建设工程、个性化定制和DIY产品自制等诸多方面,正向着大尺度、精致化、自动化方面大踏步跨进。

52. Additive manufacturing, namely 3D printing, is a new type of intelligent industry. It is a major change in the manufacturing method. It plays an invaluable role in realizing product intellectualization, accelerating research and design, reducing material consumption and improving work efficiency. 3D printing is widely used in many

aspects such as new product design, mold development, construction engineering, specialization and DIY product customization, and it is striding forward towards a large scale, refinement and automation.

(四)产业智能化

Industrial Intellectualization

53.智能化的主体是产业智能化,旨在智能新技术在各行各业的广泛应用,将爆发巨大的产业能量。"互联网+"仅是前奏,从互联网到智能网是重大升级,实施"智能+""人工智能+"才是主题。互联网传递数据,智能网将数据转化智能,实现系统的最优解。智能与产业的高度融合,其本质是智能赋能于实体经济,成为经济发展的全新生产力。

53. The main body of intellectualization is industrial intellectualization, which is aimed at the wide applications of intelligent new technologies in various industries and will generate huge industrial energy. "Internet+" is only a prelude. Transformation from the Internet to the intelligent network is a major upgrade. The implementation of "smart+", "artificial intelligence+" is the theme. The Internet transfers data, and the intelligent network transforms the data into intelligence to achieve the optimal solution of the system. Integration of

intelligence and industry is based on the fact that intelligence is empowered in the real economy and becomes a new productive force for economic development.

54.智能制造为新制造，对产业智能化起到重要作用。智能制造的关键是工业互联网，工业互联网的应用为大系统工程，包括五大板块：一是智能产品，应用芯片等技术实现产品的智能；二是智能开发设计，采用大数据技术和仿真技术进行智能化设计；三是智能供应链，在云平台上解决供应链的高效协同运行；四是智能生产，在采用机器人技术基础上，实施定制化和分布式柔性生产；五是智能服务，通过软件为用户提供智能服务和远程监控。五大板块构建智能制造的整体解决方案，其核心是数据流主导业务流、实物流、资金流，从而实现数据流的一体化运营。

54. Intelligent manufacturing is a new manufacturing and is the primary application of industrial intellectualization. The key to intelligent manufacturing is the industrial Internet. The application of the industrial Internet is big systematic engineering, including five major sectors: first, intelligent products. Application chips and other technologies help achieve product intelligence. Second, intelligent development and design. Big data technology and simulation technology are used for intellectualized

design. Third, the intelligent supply chain, which delivers the efficient and coordinated operation of the supply chain on the cloud platform. Fourth, intelligent production. Based on the use of robotics technology, customized and distributed flexible production are implemented. Fifth, intelligent services, which provides users with intelligent services and remote monitoring through software. The five major sectors draw an overall solution to intelligent manufacturing. The core is that the data flow leads the business flow, real logistics, capital flow to achieve integrated operation of data flow.

55.智能商业为新零售,发展非常迅速,创新不断加快。从电子商务开始到智能零售再到无人商店,新零售带来历史性的商业大变革。新零售有三大特点:一是体验化,始终以客户为中心,将交易变成服务,强化体验第一,注重客户社交、高效智能支付,在消费场景打造可视化的休闲生活空间;二是一体化,重在业务在线,实施门店、网点、微店三店同步,线上线下一体化经营;三是数据化,人、货、场相互连接,不断产生数据,由数据驱动业务,重在提高效率,实现千人千面的个性化服务。

55. Intelligent business is a new retail, which enjoys rapid development and increasing innovation. From e-commerce to intelligent retail to self-service stores, new retail brings

historic business revolution. The new retail has three major characteristics：first，experience. Always customer-centered，it turns transactions into services，strengthens experience first，focuses on customer socialization，efficient intelligent payment，and creates a visual leisure living space in the consumption. Second，integration. It focuses on business online，implements simultaneous operation both online and offline of stores，outlets，and online microshops. Third，dataization. People，goods，and farms are connected to each other，and data is continuously generated. Data-driven business is focused on improving efficiency and achieving personalized services for thousands of people.

56.智能农业为新农业，它广受欢迎，围绕农业产业链，从插秧、施肥、种植、植保、灌溉、收割到养殖全方位实施智能化。同时从农产品加工到成品，进行全过程溯源管理，以确保食品安全。智能实现农业精准化，对提高农业生产力意义重大。

56. Intelligent agriculture is a new agriculture，and agricultural intelligence is very popular. Around the agricultural industrial chain，it is intelligent in all aspects from transplanting，fertilizing，planting，plant protection，irrigation，harvesting and breeding. At the

same time, during the process of agricultural products to the finished products, the whole process traceability management is carried out to ensure food safety. Intelligently achieving agricultural precision is of great significance for improving agricultural productivity.

57.智能金融为新金融,其重心是金融科技,主要包括金融大数据、移动数字支付、数字信用、区块链、智能投顾、数字货币等新技术,已广泛应用于金融业中的银行、保险、证券、投资、融资、期货、租赁、资管、理财等业务领域。金融本质上是数据产业,更适应于智能新技术,特别是人工智能技术,对满足客户定制服务、提高资本效率、降低金融风险等方面,创造极其重要的价值。

57. Intelligent finance is a new finance, with a focus on financial technology, including financial big data, mobile digital payment, digital credit, blockchain, robo-advisor, digital currency and other new technologies. It has been widely used in banks, insurance, securities, investment, financing, futures, leasing, asset management, wealth management and other business aspects in the financial field. Finance is essentially a data industry, and it is more suitable for intelligent new technologies, especially artificial intelligence technologies, to create extremely important value for satisfying customized services,

improving capital efficiency, and reducing financial risks.

58. 智能能源为新能源,太阳能、风能、水能、地热能等可再生能源发展迅速,由于新能源具有分布式、大规模、不稳定、不协同等特点,必须建设新能源微电网。微电网中新能源最大的“痛点”是价格高,需要政策补贴。通过全面智能可使微电网系统整体最优化,从而大幅度降低电价,实现平价上网,确保新能源可持续发展。

58. Intelligent energy is a new energy source. The renewable energy sources such as solar energy, wind energy, hydro energy and geothermal energy are developing rapidly. Due to the distributed, large-scale, unstable and non-cooperative characteristics of new energy sources, it is necessary to build a new energy microgrid. The biggest “pain point” for new energy in the microgrid is the high price and the need for policy subsidies. Through comprehensive intelligence, the microgrid system can be optimized as a whole, thereby greatly reducing electricity prices, achieving fair price Internet access, and ensuring sustainable development of new energy.

59. 智能交通为新交通,实现汽车智能是人类的长期愿望。汽车发展方向要电动化、智能化、网联化和共享化,这四个“化”都离不开智能化。特别是汽车驾驶已从智能汽车走向智能驾驶，未来逐步走向无人驾驶，人工智能是实现无人驾驶的最佳途径。智能网联汽车将实现全面云化。

59. Intelligent transportation is a new transportation, and achieving automotive intelligence is a long-term desire of mankind. The automobile development must be electrified, intelligent, networked and shared. These four trends are inseparable from intellectualization. In particular, car driving has moved from smart cars to smart driving, and the future is gradually moving towards driverlessness. Artificial intelligence is the best way to achieve driverless driving. Intelligent networked cars will fully be on cloud.

60. 智能医疗为新医疗，新医院正在向全面智能方向发展，各项业务不断电子化、自动化，实现精准医疗。现在机器智能开始帮助医师治病，成为辅助医生。美国已建造人工智能“超级医生”和“虚拟病人”，通过机器学习优秀医师的经验和技能，成为高水平的全科医生，指导培训初级医生，模拟治病提升医术水平，智能医疗为人类带来新的福音。

60. Smart medical care is new medical care, and new hospitals are developing towards comprehensive intelligence. All businesses are continuously electronic and automated

to achieve precise medical care. Now machine intelligence begins to help doctors cure and become assistant doctors. The United States has built artificial intelligence "super doctors" and "virtual patients" to learn the experience and skills of excellent physicians through machine learning, to become a high-level general practitioner, to guide the training of junior doctors, to simulate treatment and improve medical skill. It is apparent that intelligent medical care brings benefits to human beings.

61. 智能家居为新家居，家居智能化是人们对居住场景的一种向往。家居中所有家具和物件都可以应用物联网和无线通信(WiFi)成为智能终端，智能家居依托家庭互联网提供智能服务。随着家庭智能助理和服务机器人的应用，智能家居在云端，将成为广大居民实现高效、方便、舒适和安全的智能化美好生活的方式。

61. Intelligent home is a new home, and home intelligence is a yearning of people in living scenes. All furniture and objects in the home can be applied to the Internet of Things and wireless fidelity (WiFi) become intelligent terminals. Intelligent home rely on the home Internet to provide intelligent services. With the application of home assistants and service robots, intelligent homes in the cloud will become an intelligent and beautiful life for the

residents to achieve efficiency, convenience, comfort and security.

62. 智能服务为新业态服务，主要方式是在线服务，包括在线办公、在线会议、在线客服、在线咨询、在线运维、在线监管、在线诊疗、在线救助等，通过大量动态数据，实施精准监控。在线服务最为成功的是在线教育，数以万计的人在云端“慕课”学习，不断更新知识和技能，特别是农村和偏远地区的学生都可以得到优质教学资源和服务。

62. Intelligent services serve the new business forms. The main methods are online services, including online office, online conference, online customer service, online consultation, online operation and maintenance, online supervision, online diagnosis and treatment and online rescue. A large number of dynamic data helps establish accurate monitoring. The most successful online service is online education. Thousands of people study "MOOC" in the cloud and constantly update their knowledge and skills. Especially in rural and remote areas, students can get quality education resources and services.

63. 智能城市是智能新技术的社会化综合应用。建设智能城市要在搞好顶层设计的基础上，把握好三大关键：一是以数为基，智能城市的基础在数据，首先要将城市中所有数据大集中，建立数字大脑，为全社会所共享。二是以人为本，智能城市的宗旨要从人的需求出发，一切为人服务好。三是以民生为要，将民生中最需要的医、食、住、行、安全、环境等作为重中之重，实施智能化发展。

63. Intelligent city is a comprehensive application of intelligent new technologies. To build an intelligent city on the basis of doing a good job of top-level design must grasp the three key points: first, based on the data. The basis of the intelligent city is the data. The first thing to do is to gather all the data in the city, establish a digital brain shared by the whole society. Second, people-oriented. The purpose of the intelligent city is to start from the needs of people and serve people. Third, focus on people's livelihood. The most important elements like medicine, food, housing, transportation, security, and environment should be given the highest premium and intelligent development should be implemented.

五、智能新企业

Intelligent New Enterprises

(一)企业全面智能

Corporate Comprehensive Intelligence

64.建设全面智能企业是一场深刻变革，对于企业发展具有战略意义。企业全面智能应遵循三大原则：第一用户为纲，用户本位是企业之纲，智能化始终要将用户放在首位，一切围绕用户需求而为。第二规划为先，智能化首先要整体规划，搞好顶层设计，加强系统化建设。第三问题为要，以问题为导向，逐步推进智能化建设。提高企业数字化能力，特别要重视人的因素，这是实现全面智能的核心所在。

64. Building a comprehensively intelligent enterprise is a profound change that is strategic for the corporate development. The enterprise's comprehensive intelligence should follow three principles: first, user as the guideline. The user standard is the enterprise's guideline. The intellectualization always has to put the users first, and everything should be centered around the users' needs.

Second, plan as the first. Intellectualization must first be planned as a whole, do a good job in top-level design, and strengthen systematization. Third, issue as the focus. Problem should be oriented to gradually promote intellectualization. Improving the digitalization capabilities of enterprises, especially the human factors, is the core of achieving comprehensive intelligence.

(二)互联企业

Interconnected Enterprises

65.互联是智能企业的前提,打造互联企业至关重要,互联越多,资源越多,机会也就越多。互联企业首先是企业内部互联,将部门、人员、机器、设备、物件等互联互通,连接产生交互,交互促进协同,协同创造价值。最好的联结器是微信,要将微信作为新的管理工具,充分发挥微信联结人的作用,为企业管理提供新的服务。

65. Interconnection is the premise of intelligent enterprises. It is essential to build interconnected enterprises. The more interconnections, the more resources, the more opportunities. The interconnected enterprise is firstly interconnected within the enterprise, interconnecting departments, personnel, machines, equipments, and objects, connecting to create interactions, which will promote synergy, and in result,

value is synergistically created. The best connector is WeChat. WeChat should be used as a new management tool to fully utilize the role of WeChat in connecting people to provide new services for enterprise management.

66.互联企业的外部联结同样重要，主要将企业外部的用户、供应商、合作商以及利益相关者实现互联互通，其中用户的联结要放在首位，进而向跨界开放式互联，形成企业生态系统。优秀企业要打造无边界企业：一方面，大大提高供应链效率，降低协作成本，创造用户更好价值；另一方面，大大拓展产业生态空间，实现企业更大发展。

66. The external connection of the interconnected enterprise is equally important. It mainly connects users, suppliers, partners and stakeholders outside the enterprise. The connection of users should be placed in the first place, and then open interconnection to the cross-border should be made to form the corporate ecology. Excellent enterprises must create borderless enterprises. On one hand, they will greatly improve the efficiency of supply chain, reduce the cost of cooperation, and create better value for users. On the other hand, they will greatly expand the industrial ecological space and realize greater development of enterprises.

(三)在线企业

Online Enterprises

67.在线是智能企业的关键,企业的所有业务都应该在线。由于线上成本低、效率高,凡是能在线上做的业务尽量不要在线下做。最先在线的业务是营销,网络营销如雨后春笋般蓬勃发展,电子商务爆发力强,为企业开拓巨大的市场新空间。电子商务仅是业务在线的一个环节,应将电子商务扩展为商务电子,商务电子是将所有线下业务全部上线,在互联网上开拓发展,实现企业商务全程电子化。

67. The key to an intelligent business is to be online, and all business should be online. Due to the online low cost and high efficiency, all businesses that can go online are not allowed to go offline. The first online business is marketing. Internet marketing has sprung up, and e-commerce has a strong explosive force, opening up a huge new market space for enterprises. E-commerce is only a link of business online. E-commerce should be extended to business electronics. Business electronics is to bring all offline businesses online, explore and develop on the Internet, and realize the full electronicization of corporate business.

68.企业业务在线的基本模式是"O2O",线下"O"为业务,线上"O"为数据,中间"2"为融合,线上流量往下移,线下的数据往上移,线上与线下实现一体化。实施“O2O”模式关键是“2”,线上与线下不能相分离,不是各自独立运营,一定要相互融合,通过互动成为一体。

68. The basic mode of corporate business online is “O2O”, in which, the offline “O” is the business, the online “O” is the data, the middle “2” is the fusion. The online flow moves downward, and the offline data moves up so as to achieve integration between online and offline. The key to implementing the “O2O” mode is “2”. The online and offline cannot be separated. They do not operate independently. They must be integrated with each other through interaction.

69. 企业在线首先是“上网”,进而是“上云”,即跨上云计算平台,实施全面云化。信息化的IT架构应走向云架构,企业内部要用云服务,也可以用外部云服务。工业时代发展要增加用电量和用水量,智能时代发展要增加用“云量”和用“数量”。未来大企业都在云上,线下是大量分布式小企业,线上在云端聚集成大企业,打造大型新企业的联合舰队。

69. The first thing for the enterprise to go online is to go “on the Internet” and then “up to the cloud”, that is, to get on the cloud computing platform and implement a comprehensive cover of cloud. Informatized IT architecture should move toward a cloud architecture.

Enterprises should use cloud services both inside and outside. In the industrial era, development called for more electricity consumption and water consumption. In the intelligent era, the use of "cloud" and "quantity" should be increased. In the future, large enterprises are all on the cloud, and there will be a large number of distributed small enterprises offline. They are integrated into large enterprises on the Internet to build a joint fleet of large new enterprises.

70. 在线是全新的工作场景，由于互联网的发展，创造了"平台＋个人"的新型工作方式。当今大量知识工作者在互联网和云平台上工作，建立自己的云工作室，成为自由工作者。现代企业应有两类员工：一类是在册员工，固定在企业工作；另一类是在线员工，众包为企业工作。其实能人皆在线上，网络上有高手，可为企业创造更多更好的价值。

70. It is wholy new to work online. Due to the development of the Internet, a new way of working "platform＋individual" has been created. Today, a large number of knowledge workers work on the Internet and cloud platforms, building their own cloud studios and bccoming frcclancers. Modern enterprises should have two types of employees, one is registered employees, fixed in

the enterprises; the other is online employees, crowdsourcing for the enterprises. In fact, everyone can be online. There are experts on the Internet, who can create more and better values for the enterprises.

(四)数据企业

Data Enterprises

71. 数据是智能企业的基础,无数不智。企业智能首先要数据大集中,建立大数据中心,凡是企业的数据,所有部门和个人都要统一管理,实现数据共享。基础数据固然重要,更为重要的是业务数据和用户数据,特别是动态即时数据尤为宝贵。数据集中后,应进行清洗整理为有效数据,进入数据仓库为企业开发使用。

71. Data is the foundation of intelligent enterprises. No data is unwise. Enterprise intelligence must first gather data and establish a big data center. All enterprise data, whether belongs to the department or the individual, must be managed in a unified manner to achieve data sharing. Basic data is important indeed, but business data and user data are of greater importance, especially the dynamic real-time data. After the data is collected, it should be cleaned up into valid data and enter into the data warehouse for corporate development and use.

72.数据驱动业务是智能经济的最大特征，企业所有业务都要数据化，通过传感器、射频器件、二维码、电子标签等将人员、产业、设备、原料、能源等生产要素集成为数据包，由数据来驱动业务。所有流程中，数据流处于首位，由数据流主导业务流，业务流主导实物流，实物流主导资金流，实现四流一体化。

72. The data-driven business is the biggest feature of the intelligent economy. All businesses must be digitalized. Integrate production factors such as personnel, industry, equipment, raw materials, and energy will be transformed into data packets through sensors, RF devices, QR codes, and electronic tags so that business will be driven by data. In all processes, the data flow is in the first place as the data flow dominates the business flow; the business flow dominates the real logistics; and the real logistics leads the capital flow, realizing the four-stream integration.

73.重新定义企业，当今许多大企业都将自己定义为数据企业，这是时代的新要求。数据在企业中处于基础地位，所有企业都要建立数据机构，设立首席数据官(CDO)和数据总监等岗位，这要成为企业的标配，统一管理开发大数据。同时要培育好数据人才，从领导、管理层到员工都要学习数据知识和技能，不断提高企业开发应用数据的能力。

73. Redefine the enterprise. Many of today's large

enterprises define themselves as data ones, which is a new requirement of the times. Data is at the foundation of the enterprise. All enterprises must establish data institutions and set up positions such as chief data officer (CDO) and data director, who will manage and develop the big data. This should become the standard of the enterprises. At the same time, we must cultivate good data talents. All personnel from leaders, managers to employees should learn data knowledge and skills, and continuously improve the ability of enterprises to develop application data.

74. 数据是资源,更是资产。数据资产包括大数据、数字内容、软件系统、APP、小程序、网站、公众号、微博、微信、二维码、虚拟货币等。企业长期积累的数据资产十分宝贵,为企业的重要知识财富。通过区块链技术,数据资产可以创造、交换、转让,更能不断增值和变现,实现数据资产证券化。数据资产日益增长,将超过实体资产,成为企业最大的新资产。

74. Data is a resource and an asset. Data assets include big data, digital content, software systems, APPs, applets, websites, official accounts, Weibo, WeChat, QR codes and virtual currency. The long-term accumulation of data assets is very valuable knowledge wealth for enterprises. Through blockchain technology, data assets can be

created, exchanged, and transferred, and more value-added and realized to achieve data asset securitization. Data assets are growing and will surpass physical assets and become the company's largest new asset.

六、新经济组织

New Economic Organizations

(一)组织大变革

Great Organizational Change

75.新经济推动组织大变革,创造新型组织。传统企业为金字塔组织,纵向科层结构,以层级控制为主,内部相对封闭。新经济企业为网络式组织,横向网络结构,以互相协作为主,内外开放边界。扁平化的网络使组织信息传递快,联结互动多,经营活力大,成为具有强大生命力的新型经济组织。

75. The new economy is driving organizational change and creating new types of organizations. The traditional enterprise is a pyramid organization. The vertical bureaucratic structure is mainly based on hierarchical control, and the interior is relatively closed. The new economic enterprises are network-based organizations

with horizontal network structures. Mutual cooperation is the mainstay, and internal and external boundaries are open. The flat network makes the organization information transfer fast, the connections interact more, the business more vital so as to become a new economic organization with strong vitality.

(二)社群化组织

Community Organization

76.数字新经济的组织基础是社群,社群为新型社会化组织,由群有相同兴趣爱好或共同目的的人群组成,成为自由人的联合体。社群的重要组织形式是微群,通过微信将人群组合成为微群,利用公众号等进行活动。社群组织有三大功能:第一,社群是智库,社群中的群主和成员富有智慧和技能,成为新型大智库;第二,社群是市场,社群中的人群有各种需求和价值,成为新型大市场;第三,社群是财富,社群成员的大量财富有待挖掘,成为新型大金矿。

76. The organizational foundation of the digital new economy is the community. The community is a new type of social organization. It is composed of a group of people with similar interests or common purposes and becomes a combination of free people. The important organizational

form of the community is micro-groups, which are formed through WeChat, and activities are carried out through official accounts. Community organizations have three major functions: first, the community is a think tank. The group owners and members in the community are smart and skilled. It is a new type of think tank. Second, the community is the market, and the people in the community have various needs so it becomes a new type of big market; Third, the community is wealth. The wealth of members of the community has yet to be tapped into a new type of big gold mine.

77. 社群营销是新型营销方式,利用社群开发市场大有可为,用户社群化是大势所趋。社群营销与传统营销相比有根本性变化,集中起来为四个不营销:一是无体验不营销,社群营销以体验为根本。二是无社交不营销,社群营销的重心在于社交活动;三是无移动不营销,社群营销通过手机来实现;四是无服务不营销,社群营销以服务为中心,交易只是服务的结果。

77. Community marketing is a new type of marketing. The use of community for market development is promising, and user community is the general trend. Compared with

traditional marketing, community marketing has fundamental changes, focusing on four non-marketing: first, no experience, no marketing. Community marketing is based on experience. Second, no social, no marketing. The focus of community marketing lies in social activities. Third, no mobile, no marketing. Community marketing is achieved through mobile phones and WeChat. Fourth, no service, no marketing. Community marketing is service-oriented, and transactions are only the result of services.

78.微商是全新的社会营销力量,具有强大的生命力,已形成数量可观的新型营销大军。微商利用自行组织的微群直接面向客户,特别是"网红",通过自媒体应用专业知识开展营销,创造了许多新模式新业态。微商为"四者合一",既是消费者,也是传播者,又是服务者,更是创业者。微商队伍不断扩大,必须提高自身素质,培育职业道德和专业技能,逐步向职能化发展,为企业营销发挥不可替代的积极作用。

78. WeChat Business is a brand-new social marketing force with strong vitality and has formed a large number of new marketing personnel. WeChat Business uses self-organized Wechat groups to directly target customers, especially the

Internet celebrities, and carrys out marketing through professional knowledge of We media application so that it has created many new models and new business forms. WeChat Business is a "four-in-one", which is a consumer, a communicator, a server, and an entrepreneur. The WeChat Business team is constantly expanding. It is necessary to improve its own quality, cultivate professional ethics and professional skills, and gradually develop into functionalization to play an irreplaceable positive role in corporate marketing.

(三)自驱动组织

Self-driven Organizations

79. 新经济引导企业进行内部市场化改革,把基本立足点放在搞活企业细胞上,自驱动组织为必由之路。自驱动组织的基本模式是"大平台+小团组",企业上层为大平台,主要四大职能为:战略、赋能、协同和监管。企业基层为小团组,组织最小经营单元。小团组为利润主体,责权利紧密结合,直接面向用户,在企业内部创业发展成为自主经营体。

79. The new economy guides enterprises to carry out internal market-oriented reforms, and puts a basis on invigorating corporate cells. Self-driven organization is the

only way. The basic mode of self-driven organizations is "big platform + small group". The upper level of enterprises is the big platform, whose four major functions are: strategy, empowerment, coordination and supervision. The grassroots level of the enterprise is the small group and the smallest business unit of the organization. The small group is the main body of profit. The rights and responsibilities are closely combined, directly facing the users. The entrepreneurial development within the enterprise becomes an independent business.

80. 自驱动组织的经营机制在于自组织。传统组织是绿皮火车，火车跑得快，全靠车头带，动力全在车头上，车头就像企业领导，员工坐在车厢中。自组织是高铁动车，动车的车头没有动力，只管前进方向和车厢协同，动力全在车厢中，每节车厢都有发电机和电动机，实现自我驱动。绿皮火车每小时仅 70 千米，动车每小时达 300 多千米，足见自组织的巨大威力。

80. The self-driven organization's operating mechanism lies in self-organization. The traditional organization is a low-speed train. Whether the train runs fast depends on the headstock because all the power is in the heaadstock.

The enterprise leaders are the headstock and the employees sit in the carriage. Self-organization is a high-speed railway train, where the headstock has no power but only takes charge of the direction and the coordination. All the power is in the carriages, each of which has a generator and motor to achieve self-driving. The low-speed train runs at only 70 kilometers per hour while the high-speed railway train runs more than 300 kilometers per hour, which shows the great power of self-organization.

(四)"双合"组织

Organizations with Partnership and Cooperation

81. 所谓"双合"组织就是对内合伙对外合作。企业发展的新趋势是大企业裂变发展,小企业聚变发展。对内合伙是重要的经营机制,当今人力资本的价值已等于甚至超过货币资本的价值,对于关键性人才要引入合伙制,成为事业合伙人,构建企业命运共同体。合伙制以资本为纽带,可以人力资本入股,也可以人力资本加适当货币资本入股,还可以实行期权制和模拟分红制。合伙制改变了生产关系:从产权关系看,产权从独占制走向共有制;从分配关系看,利益从薪酬制走向分享制;从人与人关系看,人才从雇用制走向合作制。合伙制实现价值共创,风险共担,利益共享。

81. Organizations with partnership and cooperation are those which establish partnership inside and cooperation outside. The new trend of corporate development is the fission development of large enterprises and the fusion development of small enterprises. Internal partnership is an important operating mechanism. The value of human capital today equals or exceeds the value of monetary capital. For key talents, it is necessary to introduce a partnership so that they can become business partners, and build a community with shared future for the enterprise. The partnership system uses capital as a link, and can be invested by human capital. It can also be invested by human capital plus appropriate monetary capital. It can implement an option system and a simulated dividend system. The partnership has changed the production relationship: from the perspective of property rights, property rights move from monopoly to communism; from the perspective of distribution, interests move from compensation to sharing; from the perspective of people-to-people relations, talents move from employment to cooperation. The partnership realizes value creation, risk sharing and benefit sharing.

82. 新时代为合作时代，合作大于竞争是发展之道。对外合作是大势，凡是交易成本低于内部成本，都可以通过外部合作来解决。对外合作关键要选择好合作对象，选择优秀的合作者，最主要的是拥有相同的价值观。合作的纽带可以是品牌、市场、技术和资本等，合作的平台是网络，利用网络互联互通，在高效协同中共创价值。

82. The new era is the era of cooperation, and it is the way to development that cooperation is greater than competition. External cooperation is the general trend. Whenver the transaction cost is lower than the internal cost, it can be solved through external cooperation. The key to external cooperation is to choose a good object, for which, the most important is to share the same values. The bond of cooperation can be brand, market, technology and capital. The platform for cooperation is the network, which uses the Internet to achieve interconnection and creates values in efficient collaboration.

(五)“双创”组织

Innovative and Enterprising Organizations

83. “双创”即创新创业，“大众创业”“万众创新”两大经济潮流，产生大量“双创”组织。传统组织向创新组织转型难度较大，观念、组织、流程的路径依赖已经固化，打破老格局不容易。传统企业创新的途径是建立“创新中心”，在“创新中心”中，实行新理念、新人员、新机制、新技术，人员在企业内外精选，可较快取得成效。实践证明，创新要从“边缘”突破，在取得成功后逐步影响主体的创新。

83. The two major economic trends of innovation and entrepreneurship, “mass innovation, mass entrepreneurship” have resulted in a large number of innovative and enterprising organizations. It is difficult for traditional organizations to transform into innovative organizations. The path dependence of ideas, organizations and processes has been solidified. It is not easy to break the old pattern. The traditional enterprise innovation approach is to establish an “innovation center”. In the “innovation center”, new ideas, new personnel, new mechanisms, and new technologies will be implemented. The personnel will be selected inside and outside the enterprise, and the effects will be achieved quickly. Practice has proved that innovation must break through from the “edge” and gradually influence the innovation of the main body after success.

84. 创客是新经济的产物，创客团队成为创业的主体，创客运动勃然兴起，创客空间大量涌现。创业需要全方位服务，围绕创业理念，传播创业精神、创业经验和创业价值观；围绕创业资源，提供人财物产供销各种资源；围绕创业能力，引进创业导师，培训创客领导力。创业已走向社会化，大大降低创业成本，通过系统服务，打造创业生态体系，提高创业成功力。

84. Maker is the product of the new economy. The maker team has become the main body of entrepreneurship. The maker movement has risen, and the maker space has emerged in a large scale. Entrepreneurship needs a full range of services. It should disseminate entrepreneurial spirit, entrepreneurial experience and entrepreneurial values when centering around entrepreneurial ideas; it should provide resources for the supply and marketing of human resources and mterials when centering around entrepreneurial resources; it should introduce entrepreneurial instructors to train the leadership of makers when centering around entrepreneurial abilities. Entrepreneurship has become socialized, greatly reducing the cost of starting a business. An entrepreneurial ecosystem should be built through system services, to improve the entrepreneurial success.

85.独角兽是创业经济中的佼佼者，国际上对独角兽的定义：创业10年左右，企业价值超过10亿美元的公司称为独角兽；价值超过100亿美元的公司称为超级独角兽。从全球布局来看，独角兽集中在一流开发园区，主要爆发领域是智能经济、平台经济和共享经济。独角兽大部分估值出自三大产业：互联网软件、电子商务、智能硬件等，从中可见独角兽已成为新经济的摇篮。

85. The unicorn is a leader in the entrepreneurial economy. The definition of a unicorn in the world is: a company with the corporate value of more than $1 billion with a history of about 10 years; a company with a value of more than $10 billion is called Super unicorn. From the perspective of global layout, unicorns are gathered in first-class development parks. The main areas of their development are intelligent economy, platform economy and sharing economy. Most of the unicorns are valued from three major industries: Internet software, e-commerce, intelligent hardware, from which the unicorn has become the cradle of the new economy.

86.众筹是创业新工具，贯穿于创业的全过程，成为大众创业的重要法宝。众筹不光是筹资金，更为可贵的是筹资源、筹市场、筹能力。股权众筹是基本形式，更多的是业务众筹、产品众筹、服务众筹，即将业务、产品和服务作为回报。众筹要突出“众”字，参加众筹的人越多越好，每个人筹借少量资金，主要是重在参与。众筹产生大量用户资源，积累新的数据资源，一举而多得，从而满足创业的多种需求。

86. Crowdfunding is a new tool for entrepreneurship, which runs through the whole process of entrepreneurship and becomes an important magic weapon for mass entrepreneurship. Crowdfunding is not just about raising funds. What is more valuable is to collect resources, markets, and abilities. Equity crowdfunding is the basic form, and the more prevalent is business crowdfunding, product crowdfunding and service crowdfunding, namely, business, products and services as returns. Crowdfunding should highlight the word “crowd”. The more people who participate in crowdfunding, the better. Everyone raises a small amount of money with the main focus on participation. Crowdfunding generates a large amount of user resources and accumulates new data resources. One action with so many benefits meets the multiple needs of entrepreneurship.

87.创业应与资本相结合，创业企业一开始就要研究资本运作，引进创投基金、风投基金，解决创业初期的资本需求。创业进入成长期，大体有三条出路：一是坚持自我发展，创造条件上市。二是依托大企业发展，通过股份转让，与大企业共同成长。三是产业并购，将企业卖掉重新创业，创业企业就是商品，买卖企业是最大的生意。在新经济的发展中，并购成为常态，起到决定性作用。

87. Entrepreneurship should be combined with capital. Start-up businesses must study capital operation from the beginning. First, introduce venture funds and venture capital funds to solve the capital needs in the early stage of entrepreneurship. When entrepreneurship enters the growth stage, there are basically three ways out: first, adhere to self-development and create conditions for listing. Second, rely on the development of large enterprises and develop with them through the transfer of shares. Third, industrial mergers and acquisitions. Sell the enterprises to restart. Start-up businesses are commodities, and buying and selling enterprises is the biggest business. In the development of the new economy, mergers and acquisitions have become the norm and played a decisive role.

(六)全球化组织

Global Organizations

88. 新经济是全球化经济,走全球市场、全球人才、全球资源、全球生产、全球服务的新路子。全球经营应实行"三化":一要思维全球化,以全球视野、全球眼光制定全球发展战略;二要行动本土化,尽可能用本土人才、本土资源,管理好本土企业;三要全面云化,建立全球云服务平台,将世界各地分布式的经营模块在平台上协同发展,加快全球数字化进程。

88. The new economy is a global economy, taking a new path to global markets, global talents, global resources, global production, and global services. Global management should implement "three-oriented": first, we must think globally, and formulate a global development strategy with a global vision and a global perspective. Second, we must act locally, which means we should use local talents and local resources to manage local enterprises. Third, we must build a full cover of cloud. It is necessary to stablish a global cloud service platform, and coordinate the development of distributed management modules around the world on the platform to accelerate the global digitalization process.

七、新时代领导力

Leadership in the New Era

(一)以人为本

People-oriented

89.新时代引领新经济，新经济需要新的领导力。新领导力的宗旨是以人为本，改变传统以物为本的领导方式。由于互联网的发展，一个人可以联结整个世界，个体的力量迅速崛起，每个都是“小宇宙”，具有强大的爆发力。以人为本，首先要依靠人，充分发挥人的聪明才智；同时要为了人，一切为人的发展服务。

89. The new era leads the new economy, which requires new leadership. The purpose of the new leadership is to be people-oriented and to change the traditional material-oriented leadership. Due to the development of the Internet, a person can connect to the whole world, and the strength of the individual rises rapidly. Everyone is a "small universe" with an explosive power. People-oriented means we must rely on people to give full play to people's

intelligence and at the same time, serve people for their development.

90. 当今时代,新生代即80后、90后、00后逐步成为社会的主体,90后和00后合起来号称为9000岁,是最富活力的社会群体。这个群体生活在互联网时代,他们文化程度高,自我意识强,发展潜力大。新的领导力要面对新生代的成长,新生代大多是知识群体,区别于传统的劳务群体,要从注重胜任力为主转向注重创造力为主,创造力是最为宝贵的,应最大限度发挥新生代的创造潜能。

90. In the modern era, the new generations, namely, the post-80s, the post-90s and the post-00s are gradually becoming the main body of the society. Called 9000 after combination, the group of the post-90s and the post-00s is the most dynamic social group. Living in the Internet era, This group is the original citizen of the Internet. They have a high level of education, strong self-awareness and great potential for development. The new leadership must face the growth of the new generations. The new generations are mostly knowledgable groups. Different from the traditional labor groups, their focus turns from competence to creativity. Creativity is the most valuable and it should be maximized to give full play to the creative potential of the new generations.

(二)创新为纲

Innovation as the Guideline

91. 新经济本质上是创新型经济,新经济以创新为纲,为创新劳动的代表,创新的意义超过以往任何历史时期。创新呼唤新的领导力,要从领导劳务员工为主转向领导知识员工为主,从组织资源型加工型经济为主转向组织知识型科技型经济为主,从管理物质生产为主转向管理数字生产为主,以适应新经济发展的内在需求。

91. The new economy is essentially an innovative economy. The new economy takes innovation as its guideline and represents the innovative labor. The significance of innovation is more than in any other historical period. Innovation calls for new leadership. It is necessary to transform from leading labors to leading knowledgable workers, from organizing resource-based processing economy to organizing knowledge-based or technology-based economy, from managing material production to managing digital production to adapt to the inherent needs of the new economic development.

92. 创新的根本在于人才,重点培育两类人才:一是创新型企业家,企业家的使命就是创新。现代企业要从企业家个体领导走向团队领导,培育创新意识强烈的企业家团队。二是创新型专业人才,专业人才应富有现代新知识和新技能,培育学习能力强的新型技术人才和管理人才,特别是复合型人才。

92. The root of innovation lies in talents, focusing on cultivating two talents: first, innovative entrepreneurs, whose mission is innovation. Modern enterprises must move from individual leadership to team leadership and foster a team of entrepreneurs with a strong sense of innovation. Second, innovative professionals. Professional talents should be rich in modern new knowledge and new skills. It is vital to cultivate new types of technical and management talents with strong learning abilities, especially compound talents.

93. 创新的关键在于制度创新,在实践中制度创新高于技术创新。创新的本质是试错,需要建立两大新机制:一要容忍失败,失败是成功的副产品,全社会要形成鼓励创新容忍失败的新机制;二要保护创新,对于创新的成果要严格保护,加强知识产权的保护制度。对于创新人才更需强化保护。

93. The key to innovation lies in institutional innovation, in which institutional innovation is higher than technological innovation. The essence of innovation is trial and error. Two new mechanisms need to be established: first, failure should be tolerated since failure is a by-product of success, and the whole society must form a new

mechanism in which failure is tolerated by innovation. Second, we must protect innovation, strictly protect the results of innovation, and strengthen the protection system for intellectual property rights. For innovative talents, it is necessary to strengthen protection.

(三)赋能为基

Empowerment as the Foundation

94.工业时代的管理以控制为主,组织流程乃至人员长期固化,过度管理方式制约了人们的积极性和创造性。新经济时代要重新定义管理,将管理变成服务,将控制变成赋能。赋能的内涵为三大赋能:一是赋权力;二是赋资源;三是赋本领。赋能为基,应实现人性化管理,回归人的本性,使人具有更大的自由度和灵活性。硅谷给予员工每周20%的自由时间,大大激发了员工的创造力,为企业实现全新的价值。

94. Management in the industrial age is dominated by control. Organizational processes and even the personnel are solidified for a long time. Excessive management restricts people's enthusiasm and creativity. In the new economic era, we must redefine management, turn management into service, and turn control into empowerment. The connotation of empowerment is the three major ones: firstly, the empowerment of powers;

secondly, the empowerment of resources; thirdly, the empowerment of abilities. Based on empowerment, natural empowerment of human rights, and the return to human nature should be achieved to give people greater freedom and flexibility. Silicon Valley gives employees 20% free time per week, which greatly motivates employees' creativity and creates new values for the company.

(四)量子领导

Quantum Leadership

95.最新的领导理论为量子领导,量子领导的核心是量子思维。量子是相对原子而言的,原子是固定的、稳定的,量子是变化的、随机的。量子学认为物质的最小单元是弦,弦是振动的频率,具有很大的不确定性,可以通过概率来确定,在不断的试验中提高概率。当今时代具有量子特征,即不确定性处于混沌失控状态,主要表现为多变、快速和复杂,不确定性原理已渗透到经济和社会的方方面面。现代领导应具有量子思维,适应不确定性的新常态,确立联系、动态和开放的大思维,增强概率和弹性新意识,以提升新的领导力。

95. The latest leadership theory is quantum leadership, and the core of quantum leadership is quantum thinking. Quantum is relative to atom. The atom is fixed and stable while quantum is random. Quantum science believes that

the smallest unit of matter is the chord, which is the frequency of vibration, with great uncertainty, which can be determined by probability and the probability is increased in continuous experiments. The current era has quantum characteristics, that is, the uncertainty is in the state of chaos, mainly manifested as changeable, fast and complex. The principle of uncertainty has penetrated into all aspects of the economy and society. Modern leaders should have quantum thinking, adapt to the new normal of uncertainty, establish a big thinking of connection, dynamics and openness, and enhance the new consciousness of probability and flexibility to enhance new leadership.

96. 面对不确定性，量子领导的最大特点是拥抱变化，许多企业生于机会而死于变化。在变化面前要敢于试验，试错的成功率为50%，不试错的成功率为0，在试错纠错中发展。针对不确定性，在确定目标后，首先要敢于行动，跨出试探性的第一步，通过小步试错，对照目标，反馈迭代，不断优化，最终达成目标。从本质上讲，机器学习的方式正是如此。量子领导是时代化的新领导力。

96. In the face of uncertainty, the greatest feature of quantum leadership is to embrace change. Many companies are born with opportunities but die from changes. In the

face of change, we must dare to test. The success rate of trial and error is 50%, but the success rate of not trial and error is 0. It develops in trial and error correction. In response to uncertainty, after determining the target, we must first dare to act and take the first exploratory step. It is necessary to go through small steps of trial and error, compare the target, make feedback iterations and continuously optimize to finally achieve the goal. In essence, the way machine learning works is just like that. Quantum leadership is the new leadership of the times.

(五)新价值观

New Values

97. 价值观是新领导力的根基,价值观的创新造就新的领导力。价值观首先是认知力,领导者与领导者的竞争力的差距,最终表现为认知力的差距。认知力水平集中体现在两大方面:一是对空间价值的认知,认知潜在的价值。正如冰山一角,在水上的小冰山,大家都认知,仅为1/8,但对水下的大冰山,大家往往不认知,却为7/8,潜在价值全在于此。二是时间价值的认知,认知未来的价值。现实的价值,大家都认知,但对未来的价值,大家往往不认知,未来价值为更重要的价值,认知力的差距就在于此。

97. Values are the foundation of new leadership, and innovation in values creates new leadership. Values are

first of all cognitiveability. The gap between leaders and the competitiveness of leaders is ultimately demonstrated as the gap in cognitiveability. The cognitiveability level is manifested in two aspects: first, the recognition of spatial value, namely, the potential value. Just like the tip of the iceberg, everyone knows the small icebergs on the water which is only 1/8. But the big icebergs under water, which people often don't know constitutes 7/8. And the potential value is all here. Second, the recognition of time value and the value of the future. The value of reality is recognized by everyone, but the value of the future is often not known by people. The value of the future is more important, and it is where the gap in cognitiveability is.

98. 价值观也是学习力,学习力是领导最基本的能力。学习力有两大内涵:首先是加强知识和能力的学习,提高领导的综合素质。其次更为重要的是提高应对变化的能力。对于大潮流要主动变革,在潮流面前任何优势都是渺小的,也是脆弱的。对于风险要主动挑战,机会永远大于风险,用机会来克服风险。

98. Values are also the learning ability, which is the most basic ability of leadership. The learning ability has two major connotations: first, to strengthen the study of knowledge and ability, and improve the overall quality of

leadership. Second, it is more important to improve the ability to cope with changes. It is necessary to be active confronted with the big trend. Any advantage in the face of the trend is small and fragile. It is important to be proactive to rise up to the risks. Opportunities are always greater than risks, and opportunities should be used to overcome risks.

99. 价值观又是软实力，现在硬实力比较硬，而软实力比较软，软硬实力不匹配，最终的能力决定于软实力。正如上山，开始时体力大，很快从山脚下爬到半山腰，但在半山腰停滞了，其原因是身体上了半山腰，而灵魂仍在山脚下，人掉了灵魂当然爬不上山顶。当今，灵魂中的核心是新旧思想的矛盾，新思维成为最大的软实力。新思维正在革旧观念的命，洗旧观念的牌。中国改革开放以来，经历三次财富大洗牌，第一次是胆大的洗胆小的财富，第二次是知识多的洗知识少的财富，第三次是新思维洗旧观念的财富，现在正是第三次大洗牌。

99. Values are soft power. Hard power is now hard while soft power is soft so that soft and hard powers are not matched. But the final ability is determined by soft power. Just like climbing up the mountain, someone starts with much energy so as to quickly climb from the foot to the mountainside. But he stops because his soul is still at the

foot although his body is on the mountainside. People without a soul can not climb up to the top. Today, the core of the soul is the contradiction between old and new ideas, and the new thinking becomes the greatest soft power. The new thinking is reforming the old concepts and creating a new order. Since China's reform and opening up, it has experienced three major reshuffles of wealth. For the first time, it was the bold getting the wealth of the coward. For the second time, the knowledgeable got more wealth than the opposite ones. For the third time, the wealth is flowing from the old thinking to the new thinking and it is also where we are.

结束语：数字革命

Conclusion: Digital Revolution

100.数字革命是人类文明历史上最伟大的革命之一，带来经济和社会最为深刻的变革。数字革命使人类从低维走向高维，在高维层级上实现数字化生存和数字化发展。其本质是数字的全球化，全面建设数字基础设施，开拓数字大市场，发展数字化经济体，构建数字化社会。数字新技术的巨大作用是两大融合：第一，现实世界与虚拟世界的融合，现实世界为“阳”，虚拟世界为“阴”，成为孪生的“双胞胎”，两大世界的融合使世界变得更精彩；第二，碳基文明与硅基文明的融合，碳基文明为生物智能文明，硅基文明为机器智能文明，成为并列的双文明，两大文明的融合使世界变得更美好。数字革命起始于20世纪末叶，构建21世纪最大的新经济，到21世纪中叶将进入高级阶段，即全面智能的新时代。智能的大发展，加速社会的大进化，从更高维度开拓人类文明的全新境界。

100. The digital revolution is the greatest revolution in the history of human civilization, bringing the most profound

changes in the economy and society. The digital revolution has enabled mankind to move from low-dimensional to high-dimensional, and to achieve digital survival and digital development at the high-dimensional level. Its essence is the digital globalization. It is necessary to build comprehensive digital infrastructure, explore digital markets, develop the digitalized economies and construct a digital society. The great role of digital new technologies is two major integrations: first, the integration of the real world and the virtual world, the real world is "yang" and the virtual world is "yin", just as the twins. The integration of the two worlds makes the world become more exciting. Second, the integration of carbon-based civilization and silicon-based civilization. Carbon-based civilization is a biological intelligent civilization and silicon-based civilization is a machine-intelligent civilization, as parallel dual civilizations. The integration of two civilizations makes the world a better place. The digital revolution began in the late 20th century, trying to build the largest new economy in the 21st century. It will enter the advanced stage in the middle of the 21st century, namely, a new era of comprehensive intelligence. The great development of intelligence accelerates the great evolution of the society and opens up a new realm of human civilization from a higher dimension.

附　录

Appendix

极简元宇宙中出现的相关概念及公式说明如下。

一、元宇宙新定义

1. 元宇宙＝虚拟宇宙×现实世界＝全真数字世界

• 元宇宙既不为虚拟，又不为现实，两者之关系是相乘，而不是相加，虚实共融，成为一体；

• 全真数字世界，虚为主导，实为载体，以虚驭实，赋能实体。

2. 元宇宙是升维，从三维到高维

• 从在线到在场，进入数字新空间；

• 从上网到上链，区块链加密；

• 从 web 1.0、web 2.0 到 web 3.0，升级高维空间。

二、元宇宙新规则

1. 元宇宙组织的基本单元(Decentralized Autonomous Organization, DAO)

• 自组织：自由人的联合社区；

• 自治理：自治社区，共识机制，数字契约；

• 自创造：自由创造数字产品和资产；

• 自共享：自主共享价值，智能合约。

2. 数字内容创造方式(User Generated Content，UGC)

• DAO 中每个参与者为数字主权者，既是内容创造者，又是消费者，也是交换者；

• 人工智能 AI 也是内容创造者（AI Generated Content，AIGC）。

3. 数字价值的确权和交易(Non-Fungible Token，NFT)

• 数字资产：非同质通证 NFT，交易数字资产；

• 数字货币：通用通证，加密货币。

4. 元宇宙的进入工具，(X Reality ，XR)

• 手机：最简单工具，效果一般；

• XR：VR，AR，XR，体验沉浸；（Virtual Reality，VR Augmented Reality，AR X Reality，XR）

• 脑机接口：人脑与电脑连接，直接进入；

• 数字化身：数字人，在元宇宙中自由活动。

三、元宇宙新文明

1. 人类大迁徙，大迁徙带来大进化

• 大陆空间迁徙：智人从非洲到全球大陆；

• 海洋空间迁徙：从大陆到海洋；

• 太空空间迁徙：从陆海到太空；

• 数字空间迁徙：从物理空间到数字空间，元宇宙升维进化。

2.元宇宙价值,元宇宙的价值无限

• $V=P^N$;V 为价值,P 为节点,N 为维度;

• 价值源:每个 DAO 都是价值节点,海量 DAO,每个数据都是价值源,超级数据量;

• 新需求:元宇宙是人类新需求,全面渗透经济与社会的应用。

3.新文明,三大标志

• 数字技术的大集成,数字经济的高形态,数字社会的新空间,元宇宙实现人类进化的大跃迁——数字新文明。

后　记

Postscript

《全新数字经济》为新型文体，全书共分 7 章 35 节 100 个知识点，最后是结束语。整个文体以点为单位，100 个点都是相对独立的知识点，集成为完整的体系，既可分又可合，有利于阅读和研究。

With a new writing style, Minimalist Digital Economy is divided into seven chapters, 35 sections and 100 Knowledge points. There are concluding remarks in the end. The whole book is based on points and 100 points are fairly independent knowledge points. Integration into a complete system can either be divided or combined, which is conducive to reading and research.

为适应国际化需求，满足国外读者的需要，本书增加英文版。

In order to meet the needs of internationalization and meet the needs of foreign readers, there is also an English version of this book.

在成书过程中，我的学生南京大学吕泽琴研究生做了大量工作，在此表示衷心感谢！

In the process of writing this book, my student Lv Zeqin from Nanjing University has done a lot of work, so I would like to express my heartfelt thanks!

本著作倾注了较多的心血努力，但仍有不尽如人意之处，敬请广大读者批评指正。

I have devoted many great efforts into this book, but there are still some unsatisfactory details. I am pleased to hear your correction and suggestions.

钱志新
QianZhixin